Global Economic Optimization

Producing an Economic Miracle

By Warren H. Bellis

Acknowledgements

I offer my gratitude to the following individuals:

- My mother Marion K. Bellis whose courage and tenacity has taught me to challenge convention, and stay the course.

- My father Warren H. Bellis Sr., whose life of continuous minor miracles, engrained in me a belief in all possibilities.

- My wife Jessie whose keen mind has inspired me to consider all aspects of the subject of this book, and whose dedication to the world and its people has encouraged me to popularize this message.

- Ralph C. Taylor Jr., the most results-oriented, outside-the-box business visionary I have ever known.

- Dr. Gwen McGregor, Dr. Bill Bauman, Helen French Black, and Ken Wilber for encouraging me to think more broadly and deeply about the subject of this book.

- The many people who have expanded the awareness and discussion of Global Economic Optimization.

- Maxine Beck whose editorial genius has given more fluid expression to the ideas contained in this book.

- Jeff Harris who has advised and inspired me in the publishing of this work.

- Christian Heurich whose creative flair is evident in the cover of this book.

Dedication

As is stated by many eastern and western philosophical traditions
*"He who thinks he knows, does not know. He, who thinks he does
not know, truly knows."*

As supported by the preceding, ambivalence, though viewed by some as
an indecisive and therefore weakened state of mind, can also be viewed as
a position in which judgment is suspended and opposites are allowed to
coexist.

This book is therefore dedicated to ambivalence, the fertile ground from
which holistic solutions to our multi-faceted problems may sprout.

Contents

Foreword

For more than thirty five years I have dedicated myself to the creation of value in business. The company that I founded to create value, Taylor Companies, is an investment bank headquartered in Washington, D.C., that specializes in doing acquisitions and divestitures. I feel fortunate in being able to say that the transactions completed by Taylor Companies have consistently achieved a significantly higher degree of success than those done by other investment banks and the industry at large. As many are aware, most acquisitions done in the world fail to create value and many actually destroy the value that pre-exists the transactions. The basis of our success can, I believe, be found in our focus in synergy. Synergy is the science of how to create more from what already exists, the much cited one plus one equals more than two. At the Taylor Companies we have looked deeply into the mechanics of synergy, carefully noting why it succeeds as well as the reasons why it sometimes fails to produce the intended extra value. Studying synergy like a science and then applying it methodically to acquisitions and divestitures, we have been able to expand the range of opportunities that can safely be pursued to build value. For example, our firm routinely achieves cost reducing, revenue enhancing, and PE enhancing synergies, while the industry at large focuses primarily on cost reducing synergies and is hesitant to pursue the other two categories, which are perceived as innately more risky. Yet we have employed them successfully due, I believe, to our deeper understanding of the subject.

So one could say that we have developed the science of synergy to a level beyond the norm, and I give a major portion of the credit for this development to Warren Bellis, the author of this book. Beyond being probably my closest friend, he is someone with whom I have always had a meeting of the minds. We just seem to operate on the same "wave length". In this book, Warren has provided a vision for expanding the application of synergy well beyond the usual buyer-seller relationship, to the entire global business sphere. Because synergy is the means for creating more from what already exists, the approach being suggested by Warren could create substantially more wealth than is possible with our current approach, in which the business sphere does not work together within itself and therefore deprives itself of the greater accomplishment. It can be difficult for individuals to work together, since from one perspective they are giving up their exclusive self-interest, but according to the mechanics of synergy, all involved actually gain much more than is otherwise possible. The message of Warren's book is that without increased taxes or deficit spending, the business sphere can work together and create enough additional wealth to fund solutions to the world's serious problems.

I think you will find this book to be different than any you have ever read. It presents an uncommon view of a familiar subject and may therefore require a second reading before customary views give way to this new paradigm.

Without a doubt, Warren possesses a unique vision. He is one of the most brilliant people I have ever known. He has a humble demeanor and is deeply spiritual. The combination of these traits has caused me to embrace him as a confidante and co-strategist during the course of our thirty-year business relationship. I take his book seriously because I understand the basis of its message, and because I know well its author. I hope you enjoy this book as much as I have, and enjoy getting to know the mind of Warren Bellis.

Ralph C. Taylor, Jr.
Chairman and CEO
Taylor Companies
Washington, D.C.
August 6, 2011

Preface

For nearly thirty years I have worked in the area of mergers, acquisitions, and divestitures (M&A). I am not a typical deal maker or Wall Street investment banker. For many of them, the completed deal is the crowning achievement of success. I, also, celebrate the completed deal, but relate even more to the value created by the transaction. In the M&A world I am a rarity, in that I focus deeply in one specific area of the deal—identification and quantification of the "extra value" created by the combination of two or more businesses. The extra value that is gained in combination is the amount beyond what the separate businesses can create standing by themselves. Obviously some special form of interaction must occur between the combining businesses in order to create the proverbial one plus one equals three. It is akin to a miracle in the field of business and something that has captivated my attention for nearly three decades. The firm for which I have worked has built a very successful M&A practice around the repeatability of this miracle, proactively engineering extra value into every acquisition pursued for its clients. The result has been an extraordinarily high rate of post-deal success in the performance of businesses acquired by our clients. Through my focus on the extra value in these deals, I have played a key role in this accomplishment. However, my focus is only one of the many disciplines that must be successfully orchestrated to complete a deal. Beyond the extraordinarily well-executed team work that leads to these results, the firm employs other methodologies that are as powerful as the concept of "extra value" in their contribution to the achievement of mergers, acquisitions, and divestitures for clients.

Unfortunately the concept of extra value in the field of M&A is not widely understood. Many business executives know something about it, and many claim its presence in deals they have contemplated, so as to muster support for their transactions. But, the M&A industry statistics tracked for many years, show that most completed deals did *not* create extra value and many actually decreased the pre-existing value of the businesses involved.[1] This neither surprises me nor makes me doubt the concept of extra value.

The business world simply lacks a sufficient understanding of how to facilitate the creation of extra value in a transaction. Also, more self-discipline is required so that deals known to be lacking extra value are not concluded.

My purpose here is not to dwell on the successes and failures of M&A, but is simply to share what I have come to believe as a result of my long-term experience with how companies can combine and create extra value beyond the mere sum of their stand-alone worth. Creation of extra value is possible due to the phenomenon of the whole being greater the sum of its parts (WGTSP). With the exception of the last three or four years of my career, I have looked exclusively at how this phenomenon relates to the M&A field. More recently my eyes have opened to the much broader application of the WGTSP principle in life. Whereas I previously saw it only in the context of my vocation, it now appears so integral to our existence that its sporadic absence in our lives seems far more the exception than the rule. Additionally, I have observed that where present, the WGTSP phenomenon:

- Produces the most output from the least amount of resources
- Maximizes balance within a system
- Maximizes harmony within a system

The advantages of the WGTSP effect are more relevant in light of the world's current serious economic and socio-ecological difficulties in which inefficiency, imbalance, and disharmony prevail.

My belief that mankind can jointly apply the WGTSP principle to address and solve the serious and imminent problems we are facing has prompted me to write this book presenting a detailed prescription for the application of the phenomenon to the global business sphere. My career has logically provided me with the perspectives necessary for such an undertaking. My hope is that once experts from other arenas fully grasp the significance of the WGTSP phenomenon, they will be moved to develop applications within their respective fields. At first these new approaches may be viewed with surprise and even skepticism since the world is currently confronted with so many seemingly insoluble problems. But it is our lack of understanding of the WGTSP principle that has kept us in the dark as to the possibility of re-engineering our faltering human creations to make them maximally efficient, balanced, and harmonious. The WGTSP principle is not new; we have just not yet grasped its greater significance. In light of this, I propose that the solutions have been with us all along, merely waiting for us to awaken to their presence and potential.

Introduction

Economic Problems

Three years ago the world economy was plunged into crisis. Despite indications that a recovery has begun, it will probably be some time before growth returns to pre-crisis levels. Due to continuing economic stagnancy, unemployment levels remain painfully high. The stock markets have risen significantly since their 2008 plunge but the weak recovery leaves businesses hesitant to spend the financial resources gained through overhead reductions and increased company valuations. Daunting levels of national debt lead to the obvious conclusion that we must reduce spending. This view is reinforced by the projection that, in the U.S., debt interest payments, Medicare, Medicaid, and Social Security by themselves will consume 92 cents of every federal tax dollar by 2020.[2]

We may have, for now, averted the tipping point[3] of economic disintegration, but stretching before us is a delicate road to recovery that requires us to follow the proper course to prevent a relapse. Challenging our ability to stay on course are a number of serious economic problems including continued fiscal challenges in the United States and Europe, possible slowing of China's economy, political turmoil in the Middle East, and unpredictable setbacks such as the earthquake and tsunami in Japan.[4] Our situation is especially concerning in light of the recent findings of the Davos World Economic Forum which reported that the world is suffering from a state of "global burnout syndrome" in which we have not yet regained stability in the wake of the financial crises, and do not have the strength needed to deal with our complex and interrelated problems.[5]

We must ask ourselves, are we confident of the way forward, or are we uncertain of the next move? Are we successfully steering the global economy, or are we holding on for dear life to the railings of a ship with no rudder? Because, to date, no one has unveiled a compelling master plan to insure the economic recovery and restore growth, it is fair to assume that we are in less than complete control of the situation and less than adequately prepared to navigate the months and years ahead. We are riding through volatile times in a questionable global economic vehicle. In reality, the situation is even worse than this.

Socio-Ecological Difficulties

The fragile economy is only one of many serious challenges the world is now facing. Our financial situation may be of prime concern because of the immediate pain it is creating, but great socio-ecological difficulties are gathering like storm clouds on the horizon. For example:

- Extreme weather losses are increasing more rapidly than global income. At the current rate, global bankruptcy could occur as soon as 2045.[6]

- Sea levels are expected to rise 35 inches by 2100, displacing millions of people and submerging millions of acres of land.[7]

- Other climate change-related difficulties are expected including:
  -Increased cancer, respiratory illness and other health problems[8]
  -Decreased crop yields[9]
  -Forestation losses and shifts[10]
  -Loss of bio-diversity[11]

- Fresh water supplies will be catastrophically low for 4.5 billion people by 2032.[12]

- Global-scale food shortages are likely, due to the population explosion and the growing demand for increased food quality resulting in the need for a 70% increase in farm production by 2050.[13] Predicted rainfall reductions due to climate change, as well as alternative energy-driven use of farmlands for bio-fuel production, will challenge our ability to achieve the needed increase.[14] In addition, the world is losing its fertile soil at an alarming rate of 83 billion tons annually[15], and the global bee population, crucial for fertilization of many crops, is experiencing a dramatic reduction caused by *Colony Collapse Disorder*[16].

- By 2050, there will be 2 billion more people than the Earth can safely support.[17]

- The likelihood of pandemic illness is increasing.
  -The majority of the world population now lives together in crowded urban areas.[18]
  -International travel has risen to more than 2 million people per day.[19]
  -The increased use of antibiotics is breeding "super bugs".[20]
  -Worsening conditions in areas of abject poverty increase the possibility of epidemic outbreaks.[21]
- The likelihood of international conflict is increasing:
  -There is a great disparity in the distribution of wealth in the world.[22]
  -The world is experiencing significant economic pressures.[23]
  -Scarcity of energy, food[24], and fresh water will increase.[25]
  -The number of armed conflicts is increasing each year, having doubled since 1945.[26]
- $2.2 trillion will be required over five years to repair the aging infrastructure of the U.S. alone.[27]
  -A quarter of the nations bridges are considered structurally deficient.
  -Seven billion gallons of drinking water is leaked daily.
  -Billions of gallons of untreated wastewater enter the nation's waterways annually.
- Significant ongoing threat of damage and disruption to society and the environment is posed by unpredictable occurrences of human error, technological failure, and natural catastrophes such as the 2010 oil spill in the Gulf of Mexico, and Japan's 2011 earthquake and Tsunami expected to result in losses as high as $309 billion.[28] In countries such as the United States, large national debts leave no financial reserves to respond to such costly occurrences.[29]

While seemingly isolated, these problems are actually part of an interrelated web of complex issues as is illustrated in figure 1 on the following page.

Given this interconnectedness, we cannot afford to prioritize the problems and parcel out the funding in a piece-meal fashion. Rather, we must

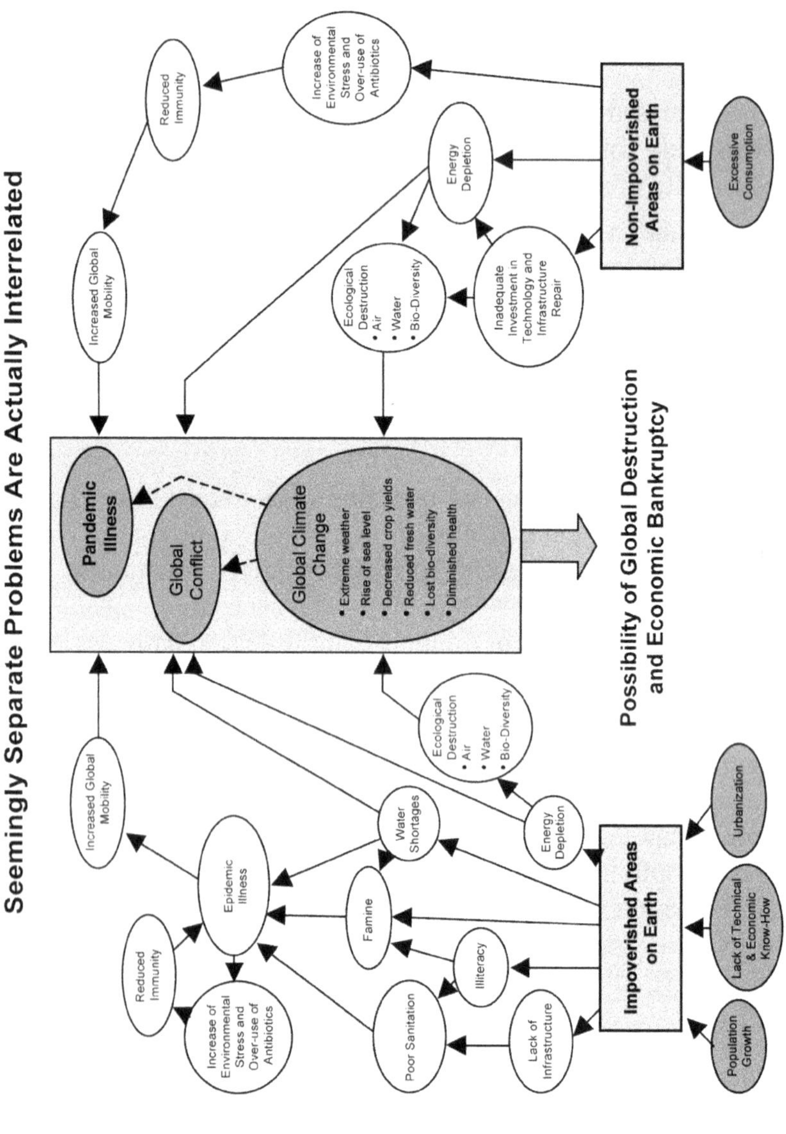
Seemingly Separate Problems Are Actually Interrelated
Pandemic Illness
Global Conflict
Global Climate Change
• Extreme weather
• Rise of sea level
• Decreased crop yields
• Reduced fresh water
• Lost bio-diversity
• Diminished health
Possibility of Global Destruction and Economic Bankruptcy
Non-Impoverished Areas on Earth
Excessive Consumption
Increase of Environmental Stress and Over-use of Antibiotics
Reduced Immunity
Increased Global Mobility
Energy Depletion
Ecological Destruction
• Air
• Water
• Bio-Diversity
Inadequate Investment in Technology and Infrastructure Repair
Impoverished Areas on Earth
Urbanization
Lack of Technical & Economic Know-How
Population Growth
Increased Global Mobility
Epidemic Illness
Reduced Immunity
Increase of Environmental Stress and Over-use of Antibiotics
Water Shortages
Famine
Illiteracy
Poor Sanitation
Lack of Infrastructure
Energy Depletion
Ecological Destruction
• Air
• Water
• Bio-Diversity

Figure 1.

employ a coordinated solution that addresses all issues and geographical locales simultaneously. Such funding costs have been estimated at hundreds of billions of dollars per year.[30]

We have been aware of these massive and complex problems for some time, but even before our present economic difficulties, adequate funding was not forthcoming from private, public, or governmental sectors.[31] Though we have not yet experienced the full impact of these problems, they deserve our immediate attention because they each have a tipping point that draws consistently closer in the absence of adequate action. What is the possibility of adequately funding solutions to these socio-ecological problems now as we struggle to recover from the economic downturn?

As is painfully obvious, sufficient funding to cover the magnitude of spending that will be necessary to bolster the economy as well as solve our socio-ecological problems, does not exist. We desperately need to generate more wealth than is currently forthcoming from our global economy, but our current approach is seriously deficient in its ability to produce the vast sums that will be required.

Fortunately, a common principle in life exists that holds the key to unlocking the world's full economic capability, a potential that greatly exceeds our present global output. Many people have undoubtedly heard the expression "the whole is greater than the sum of its parts", or *one plus one equals more than two*. Expressions of this principle are everywhere—a house is more than the sum of its materials and sub-systems, a tree is more than the sum of its bark, roots, leaves, sap, heartwood, etc., a championship football team is more than the sum of its individual players, an atom is more than the sum of its neutrons, protons, and electrons, a symphony is more than the sum of the individual instruments, the human body is more than the sum of its tissues and sub-systems.

What about the global economy? Is it also an example of the whole being greater than the sum of its parts? Currently, the answer is "no", and consequently the world's economic potential remains untapped due to the existing approach that limits the world's economic output. It is, sadly, not even equal to the sum of its parts. In today's global economy, *one plus one equals less than two*. Happily, through application of what this book refers to as Global Economic Optimization (GEO), we can unfold the world's hidden economic potential in a harmonious and balanced way, to generate the vast additional wealth needed to address our serious challenges and reset the world on the path of progress. Through this approach, we will be able to avoid deficit spending and increases in individual and corporate taxes, while generating the wealth required to:

- Solve the world's serious economic and socio-ecological problems
- Fund development of the technologies, products, and services of the future
- Raise corporate earnings to levels not possible with our current approach
- Create countless new jobs filled with purpose and mission

And while achieving these economic benefits, we will strengthen our ability to work together toward our common objectives, despite our philosophical, religious, cultural, and political differences.

But to comprehend how we might use GEO to obtain such extraordinary benefits, we must first understand the conditions necessary for the whole to be greater than the sum of its parts. Chapter One will reveal these conditions and their significance to the global economy.

Chapter One
When the Whole is Greater than the Sum of Its Parts

Although the expression *The Whole is Greater than the Sum of Its Parts* (WGTSP) is widely familiar, a wide-spread understanding of what this phenomenon is, how it works, or the degree to which it already impacts our lives remains vague. In essence, the principle states that under specific conditions, the interaction of related parts can produce a result which is greater than the mere sum of those related parts. In other words, under the right circumstances *one plus one can equal more than two*. In addition to maximizing output, examples of the WGTSP principle in action exhibit a high degree of internal balance and harmony. The world around us offers countless examples of the WGTSP phenomenon, many that are naturally occurring and others that are man-made. We will now consider several of these examples in an attempt to illustrate the standard conditions under which the WGTSP principle can work its magic.

Example 1: A Tree

Almost everywhere we look in nature, we can see spontaneously occurring manifestations of the WGTSP principle. One very common example is a tree. A tree possesses numerous distinct parts—roots, leaves, bark, sap, sapwood, heartwood, and so on. Each part has specific qualities and capabilities not characteristic of the other parts. Each part contributes a unique benefit to the tree as a whole. The various parts of the tree do not generally over shadow each other, rather they each focus on the role for which they are uniquely qualified. Each part apparently has an innate "knowledge" of how to be itself, and thereby the bark naturally manifests itself as the bark without intruding on the other parts. In addition to being in balance with those other parts of the whole tree, the bark also possesses a "knowledge" of how, beyond merely being itself, to interact in a balanced and harmonious way with the sap wood to create a tree. The result is a whole greater than the bark and the other parts standing by themselves, a healthy tree. Without this purposeful interaction of its components, the tree would be no greater than the simple sum of its parts. But, the spontaneously occurring WGTSP effect increases the overall value of the tree and its parts. To verify this, we have only to consider the image of a pile of bark, roots, sap wood, heart wood, and leaves heaped randomly on the ground, compared to the image of these elements combined in the fully formed tree.

Example 2: The Human Body

Another example of the WGTSP principle spontaneously occurring in nature is the human body. The body is comprised of numerous systems—circulatory, respiratory, endocrine, gastrointestinal, neurological, reproductive, etc. Each system is highly differentiated and contributes a unique benefit to the complete body. The various systems of a <u>healthy</u> body do not usurp each others' roles, but dedicate themselves to the unique parts for which they are solely qualified. However, each system has both an innate predisposition toward being itself <u>and</u> a sense of working in harmony with the other systems to the benefit of the whole body. Each system possesses the spontaneous inclination to interact in a balanced and harmonious way with the other systems to create and benefit the entire body. The result is a whole that vastly exceeds the sum of the individual systems in isolation. Without this purposeful interaction of the individual systems, the body could not exist.

Example 3: A Symphony Orchestra

One man-made expression of the WGTSP principle is a symphony orchestra. The orchestra contains various kinds of instruments including string, brass, percussive, and reed. The design of each instrument and ability of its corresponding musician results in production of a characteristic sound. No one instrument is played so as to drown out the sounds of the other instruments. Each musician and corresponding instrument remains coordinated in a balanced and harmonious way with the rest of the orchestra by virtue of the written score. The result is a beautifully blended piece of music that is far more enjoyable than the cacophony that would occur if the instruments were played randomly, with no attention to the score.

Example 4: A Championship Athletic Team

Athletic teams are prime expressions of the WGTSP principle. An especially pertinent one is American football where each team has numerous positions, each with a defined role for which the individual player must have specific capabilities and training. Each player is expected to focus on playing his/her position to the required level of proficiency, without usurping the roles of other positions. For example, it would be counter productive for an offensive right guard to suddenly run downfield to receive a pass, leaving the quarterback to be tackled by the onward rushing defensive linemen. By virtue of the playbook, each player has an understanding of how his/her performance on each play will complement those of the other positions. As a result each player's focus is balanced with the interests of the overall team. With consistently balanced and harmonious interaction of the positions, the team may achieve victory. Without such interaction the players would merely run randomly and ineffectively about the field.

Example 5: An Automobile

Well designed machines and equipment are also expressions of the WGTSP principle. Consider for instance an automobile that is comprised of numerous individual materials, parts, and systems, each with the specific capacities and functionalities to perform a unique role. Each component is expected to perform its function, without interfering with the operations of other parts. For instance, the cylinders in the engine must fire in a prescribed sequence, not simultaneously or randomly. The proper functioning of each part in balance with the others enables the automobile to function. The balanced and harmoniously-engineered design of the vehicle ensures that each component "knows" how to interface with the other parts in the correct way, extent, and timing so as to result in an incredibly complex implement of transportation—a whole that is vastly greater than the mere sum of the parts.

Example 6: A House

All buildings are manifestations of the WGTSP principle; for example, a house is a collection of myriad materials, devices, and systems. The floor, wall, and ceiling structures; plumbing, electrical, and mechanical systems; as well as the windows, doors, flooring, paint, and finished trim, each provide unique functionality and must deliver requisite levels of performance to create a sound structure. The plumbing system cannot make up for deficiencies in the electrical system, and the walls cannot replace the floors. Yet, based on the architect's master blueprint and the competent work of the various tradesmen, the numerous components are able to fit and function together in a balanced and harmonious way so as to produce a sound, complete home that offers refuge, security, and comfort. The finished structure has far more value than the random piles of lumber, metal, porcelain, steel, and glass that would result given no blueprint.

Example 7: Allied Victory in WWII

Some expressions of the WGTSP principle are quite simple, such as a paper coffee cup that is constructed of only two parts, the one-piece cylindrical side and the disc-shaped bottom. Alone the two are useless; together they can hold liquid. Other examples exhibit epic-scale complexity such as the allied victory in WWII. This military campaign had many separate components—millions of people in multiple countries, hundreds of participating occupations both civilian and military, and military operations on land, air, and sea, to name just a few. Each component of the war effort had a specific role to play. Civilian shipyard and factory workers, sailors, army personnel, pilots, and others were trained and relied upon to perform their distinct roles. Each participant endured enormous personal sacrifice: restrictions of occupational freedom, limitations in personal finance, and even loss of life. Sailors aboard ships did not wage land battles or fly bombing raids. Munitions manufacturers did not fire the weapons, and those on the front line did not sew their own uniforms or manufacture their own equipment. A multitude of various components were defined and coordinated by political decisions, battle plans, draft quotas, the production schedules of the factories that armed the allied war machine, and more. As a result, the roles of all contingents were coordinated in the overall war effort so as to keep the entire operation in balance. The outcome of this balanced and harmonious marshalling of such an immense volume of diverse resources was a whole far greater than the simple sum of the participating components. The WGTSP effect made possible the against-the-odds defeat of global-scale fascism and imperialism that if unchallenged, could have curtailed ordinary freedoms and dramatically changed the course of history.

This example of the Allied victory in WWII is especially significant in that it proves that even with highly complex, high-stakes, global challenges, the WGTSP principle can be applied to create critically beneficial outcomes.

Specific conditions are held in common by the previously cited examples, as well as by all other expressions of the WGTSP principle. Figure 2 illustrates this point when the characteristics as presented below are applied:

1. A through C are distinctly unique parts.
2. Each part must possess, to an acceptable degree, the capabilities as expected.
3. Each part must play its defined role to the required degree, not more or less.
4. Each part must limit itself to its prescribed role rather than usurping the roles or resources of the other parts.

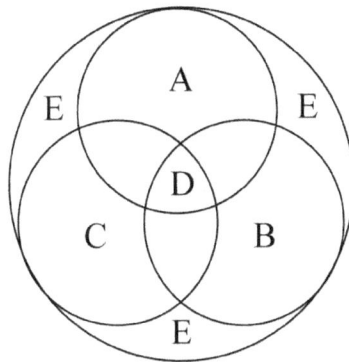

Figure 2. When the Whole is Greater Than the Sum of Its Parts

5. A balance must be maintained between the interests of the parts and the interest of the whole, with all parts sharing the vision (D) of how to interact so as to contribute to the greater whole.

6. Additional benefit (E) is produced beyond what would be possible if the preceding characteristics were not present. Production of the benefit is maximized through proper balancing of the interests of the parts with the interest of the whole, as well as through the harmonious interaction of interrelated parts.

Building on the greater clarity gained from both the preceding specific examples and the identification of the standard conditions that generally allow the whole to be greater than the mere sum of its parts, let us further broaden our consideration of the WGTSP principle in life. Upon reflection we can see that the following, when functioning optimally, are more examples of the WGTSP phenomenon.

•   All atoms, molecules, and liquids, gases, and solids comprised of molecules

•   All plants, animals (including humans), and minerals

•   All manufactured equipment, machinery, devices, and gadgets

•   All man-made systems and processes

•   All multi-person or multi-component projects or endeavors

•   All visual and auditory arts and commercial media

•   All alphabet-based languages

•   All personally, commercially, or industrially used objects that are comprised of more than one part

•   All personal, familial, social, or professional pursuits that employ team work

The importance and inclusiveness of this list certainly illustrates that the WGTSP principle is a fortunate and pervasive influence in our lives. To be sure, WGTSP and its blessings are so prevalent in the natural as well as man-made world around us, that when we really open our eyes to its existence, we quickly realize that its absence is, by far, the exception rather than the rule.

WGTSP and the Global Business Sphere

One critical exception to the rule however, involves the central message of this book. The very foundation of the world economy, the global business sphere, is seriously deficient in its adherence to the WGTSP principle. This is obvious when the previously identified conditions that accompany WGTSP, are compared to the corresponding actual conditions that exist in the global business sphere.

Conditions that Support Presence of WGTSP	Actual Conditions Present in the Business Sphere
1. There are distinct parts or components.	1. Individual firms within each industry segment are the distinct parts or components.
2. Each part must possess to an acceptable degree, the capabilities expected of that kind of part.	2. Many individual firms in the global business sphere are underperforming.
3. Each part must focus on playing its defined role to the required degree, not more or less.	3. Firms have a difficult time determining and effectively adhering to their defined roles, or core focuses.
4. Each part must limit itself to playing its prescribed role, rather than usurping the roles or resources of the other parts.	4. Through competition, firms within the same industry segment actively try to usurp one another's roles and resources and even obstruct one another's success.
5. A balance must be maintained between the interests of the parts and the interests of the whole, with all parts sharing the vision of how to interact so as to contribute to the greater whole.	5. Firms within an industry segment are predominantly self-interested and have a very limited vision of a greater whole, much less of the interaction required to achieve it.
6. Additional benefit is produced (1+1 = more than 2) beyond what would be possible if the preceding characteristics were not present. Production of the benefit is maximized through proper balance of the interests of the parts with the interest of the whole, as well as through the harmonious interaction of interrelated parts.	6. No extra value is produced beyond that of all the firms added together. In fact, a portion of each firm's gain is depleted by the demands of competition (1+1 = less than 2). This behavior prevents harmonious interaction among firms.

The Deficiencies of the Global Business Sphere

The preceding point by point comparison indicates that the global business sphere is seriously deficient in its ability to manifest the WGTSP principle and achieve the extraordinary benefits that are characteristic of this phenomenon. Examining in greater detail the nature of the deficiencies that prevent the global business sphere from expressing these benefits offers further insight. For the purposes of this WGTSP analysis as it applies to business, the individual firms within each industry segment are viewed as the parts, and the wealth generative potential of each respective industry segment is viewed as the whole that could be greater than the mere sum of the parts if the WGTSP principle were applied.

A. Documented underperformance of individual firms is widespread in the business sphere.[32] This results from deficiencies in effectively defining[33] and managing[34] the core or principal business, and in acquiring[35] and divesting the assets, resources, and capabilities needed to optimize the core business. As a result, firms are not well positioned to maximize value for their shareholders or to contribute effectively to the full realization of the wealth generative potential of their respective industry segments. Tapping into such potential would produce vast additional wealth beyond the mere sum of the outputs of the individual firms.

B. Due to the competitive dynamics that currently dominate inter-firm functioning within each industry segment, the individual firms are unable to comfortably participate in the communication and interaction needed to cooperatively produce the greater whole. This greater whole, if realized through application of the WGTSP principle, would provide the vast additional wealth needed to address our global problems. Unfortunately the business sphere's current competitive dynamics deprives us of not only the greater whole ($1 + 1$ = greater than 2), but also the savings to each firm resulting from no longer having to try to thwart the success of its competitors. Currently the competitive approach cuts into each firm's wealth output resulting in the less than optimum result ($1 + 1$ = less than 2).

Due to these deficiencies, the world is deprived of the greater wealth production, functional balance, and harmonious interaction that would occur if the conditions supporting WGTSP were fully present. Correcting this situation is of utmost importance, for doing so will generate the vast additional wealth required to:

- Solve the world's serious economic and socio-ecological problems
- Fund development of the technologies, products, and services of the future
- Raise corporate earnings to levels not possible with our current approach
- Create countless new jobs filled with purpose and mission

The remainder of this book will provide a detailed plan for adjusting the global business sphere so that it fully manifests the characteristics and benefits of the WGTSP principle.

Chapter Two
The Underperformance
of Individual Businesses

Chapter One suggested that the global business sphere should be adjusted to demonstrate the WGTSP principle and its characteristic efficiency, balance, and harmony. In considering that case, the individual firms within each industry segment would be viewed as the parts, and the whole, that could be greater than the mere sum of the parts, would be the wealth generative potential of the overarching industry segments within which the respective firms operate.

Applying the WGTSP principle would require as a pre-condition that individual firms exhibit stand-alone optimal functioning as a basis for contributing effectively to the wealth generative potential of their respective industry segments. However, currently widespread underperformance on the part of individual businesses is well documented. This deficiency of individual firms must be remedied before the global business sphere will be able to fully exhibit the greater wealth generation, harmony, and balance that accompany the WGTSP principle. But, as was suggested earlier, improving individual business performance will eliminate only one of the obstacles to the business sphere's ability to effectively demonstrate the WGTSP principle and its extraordinary benefits. The other obstacles must also be addressed and remedied. Chapter Three will discuss these necessary additional fixes.

This chapter will focus on a thorough discussion of individual firm underperformance and its remedy as an essential first step for accomplishment of the WGTSP phenomenon.

The Ideal of Business Performance

Whether as small sole proprietorships or large multinational corporations, businesses are key generators of economic value. Each business produces wealth for its suppliers, creditors, employees and shareholders. The world's wealth is largely due to the aggregate output of the world's businesses. The wealth generation of an individual business should be greatest when the firm is optimized and operating at its full potential. Three conditions must exist for an individual business to achieve optimum performance:

1. A business must have a compelling reason to exist, meaning that it must provide a product or service that is of significant value to its customers. Ideally the product or service should have enduring appeal and characteristics that differentiate it from functionally similar offerings. In addition, the business must employ the most effective means for getting the product or service into the customers' hands. These characteristics are important components of a business's core focus. This core focus is foundational, because a business must first know its essential purpose in order to define what it will and will not need in order to accomplish that purpose.

    The importance of the core is a common theme among those involved in business-related strategic thought. For example, Chris Zook who has written extensively about core focus and related strategies for growth, believes that a business's success depends significantly on effective identification of its core.[36]

2. So as to be aligned with this core focus, the business must free itself of any assets, resources, or capabilities that do not contribute to pursuit of the core. Owning such superfluous components would divert attention and financial resources away from pursuing the agreed upon compelling reason for the business to exist.

3. In addition, the business must gain possession of all assets, resources, or capabilities required for effective pursuit of the core. The business will be able to function optimally only if it has the necessary components that are properly harnessed in pursuit of the core focus.

If a business has only what it needs and nothing superfluous, it will be maximally efficient because it will consume the least assets possible while producing the greatest possible output. Maximum wealth will be generated with least cost.

In the natural course of a business' evolution, it may become necessary to pursue continued growth by using the core as a bridge into adjacent areas of business.[37] Also, in time, an originally identified focus may cease to produce viable growth and necessitate a redefinition of the core business.[38]

Given these considerations, in the normal course of pursuing business optimization, the following sequence of events might occur:

1. An initial identification of a business' core focus may indicate the need for <u>acquisition</u> of assets, resources, or capabilities for effective pursuit of the core.

2. If the rate of growth from strict pursuit of the core slackens, it may become necessary to <u>acquire</u> new assets, resources, or capabilities to effectively connect the business to areas of opportunity that are adjacent to the core.

3. If the originally identified core loses viability, a business may need to identify a new core and <u>divest</u> of the assets, resources, or capabilities that supported the old one. Also, it may need to <u>acquire</u> the assets, resources, or capabilities that will support the new core.

Therefore, in order for a business to maximize performance and resulting wealth, it must skillfully execute three core competencies:

- Effective definition/re-definition of the core
- Effective divestiture of superfluous assets, resources, or capabilities
- Effective acquisition of required assets, resources, or capabilities

A business strong in these competencies should be optimally equipped to pursue its individual potential within the limits defined by external market dynamics and regulatory guidelines. Such a business will both consume least wealth and generate the maximum wealth for its stakeholders. Clearly, a business with these three strengths strongly present will maximize its individual wealth-generative potential.

The Actual Situation Compared to the Ideal

Business-oriented researchers and strategic thinkers who have analyzed the success of the business sector have concluded that most businesses do not experience enduring success. Consider the following evidence:

- One ten-year study of 1,870 companies found that only 13% of businesses achieved even minimal profitable growth.[39]

- Analysis has indicated that, even in favorable economic conditions, nine out of ten management teams failed to grow their companies profitably.[40]

- An in-depth study of 185 companies in 33 industries conducted by Bain & Company revealed that on average almost all the profits were captured by each industry's top three competitors.[41]

- Paradoxically, the top performing companies within an industry are most likely to be performing below their optimum potential.[42]

These findings indicate that most businesses do not achieve enduring success and even the few that do are underperforming. This view indicates that substantial room for improvement exists regarding optimization of business performance. Such underperformance suggests that businesses are not doing well in the previously identified three essential skills required to maximize business achievement. The following section will discuss in detail the extent to which such impairment is actually present.

Effective Definition/Re-Definition of the Core

Initially, a business must effectively identify its core focus to optimize performance[43], but defining the core is one of the most frustrating tasks for business executives.[44] Many management teams fail to perceive the full potential of their businesses[45] and the evidence suggests that core businesses very often are undervalued.[46]

While identification of the core is generally challenging for firms, conglomerates may experience even greater difficulty[47] since by their very nature they are structured with more diverse lines of business that inherently complicate the ideal of focusing single-mindedly on an agreed upon best direction.

In time, the rate of growth from a business's defined core may decrease, necessitating the pursuit of additional opportunities. But evidence reveals that such circumstances generally create a tendency to prematurely abandon the core business rather than to find ways to extend the core's potential for growth.[48] This can be a very dangerous mistake since the core is the very source of growth and profits.[49] Rather than discarding it altogether, businesses should pursue ways to bridge from the core to adjacent areas of opportunity. Such afore mentioned adjacency moves[50] comprise six categories of expansion that are much more likely than other strategies to create growth beyond the core itself.[51] Evidence reveals that 80% of the most successful companies have used such adjacency moves to create profitable growth beyond their original cores.[52]

However, even with their greater likelihood of success, adjacency expansions succeed only 25% of the time.[53] Leading firms probably have a significantly easier time achieving success with adjacency moves because of their leadership advantages. Most notably, successful leading companies are disciplined enough to repeatedly apply the best practices of growth, including the principles governing the execution of adjacency initiatives.[54]

Businesses are typically very slow to recognize that the core has begun to lose its ability to be the foundation for a business' success[55], but timely recognition is becoming an increasingly important skill. A survey conducted with senior executives around the world revealed that the majority of them believed strategic life cycles are shortening. This indicates an increasingly shorter interval between initial core identification and the need to redefine that core.[56] Therefore, businesses must not only improve their capacity to quickly recognize the need for re-definition, but also improve their redefining of the core itself. Begun in 1994, a ten year study of the *Fortune* 500 companies indicated that nearly 60% of them experienced serious threats to their survival, and only half of them successfully redefined their cores.[57] The evidence clearly shows that widespread failure in the area of core focus definition/re-definition contributes to the general under-optimization of business.

Effective Divestiture of Superfluous Assets, Resources, or Capabilities

Non-core assets, resources, or capabilities can sometimes, but rarely, generate proportionally greater wealth than the acknowledged core business.

A product or service that is outside the core can generate comparatively high profit margins. In such cases, maintenance of the non-core focus may make sense for a period of time simply to generate the capital needed to fuel the core business. However, more often, non-core assets, resources, or capabilities do not contribute to effective pursuit of the acknowledged core focus. Therefore, retaining them will divert both financial and non-financial resources from core activities and delay growth from the core. In addition, postponement may likely result in a reduction in the magnitude of possible benefit if an issue of timeliness or a shrinking "window of opportunity" is connected with pursuit of the core.

Often businesses prolong their ownership of non-core assets, resources, and capabilities because they struggle with definition and redefinition of the core focus. If a firm does not properly identify its core focus, it cannot possibly identify the corresponding non-core business components. Such situations prohibit timely identification and divestiture of non-core components.

However, in some cases, businesses *are* fully aware of the existence of non-core assets, resources, and capabilities, and yet choose to retain them for various reasons:

- Businesses are high-paced environments where executives experience a continuous barrage of urgent demands. Such demands take priority over equally important, if not as urgent matters. Therefore, the less pressing decision to divest a non-core business component may get delayed because it is performing reasonably well and is otherwise non-problematic. The better the non-core component performs, the less likely it will be divested in a timely manner.

- Some businesses are not in significant need of raising cash or paying down debt. A more proactive management style would still press the divestiture of a non-core business component, but the lack of overall financial pressure would allow less aggressive management to put off until tomorrow what should be done today.

- Sometimes non-core components are intertwined with core components. For example, the same production facility may manufacture both core and non-core products. In many cases the non-core assets can be separated from the core, but often associated complexities cause management to temporarily delay the inevitable.

- Fear that a divestiture will not fetch the desired value for the non-core component can cause a hesitancy to act. This is especially true if the component is underperforming relative to its peers or experiencing a segment-wide low point in the business cycle.

- Uncertainty about where to invest the divestiture proceeds can sometimes weaken the resolve to move forward. This should not be a factor for a business that has a clearly defined core, but well defined cores are more the exception than the rule.

- Often a non-core business component is the brain-child of a previous acquisition strategy. Whether or not the original strategy was valid at the time, the component is subsequently viewed as non-core. Whoever authored the original strategy may still be attached to the component or reluctant to admit an earlier mistake. In such cases, the need to divest the component can go unaddressed.

- Even if the above reasons are absent, non-core business components may be retained simply because of the natural human aversion to change.

While data on the prevalence of prolonged retention of non-core business components may be insufficient, the discussion above clearly indicates that it is a significant factor contributing to the general under-optimization of business.

Effective Acquisition of Required Assets, Resources, or Capabilities

Many kinds of assets, resources, and capabilities are used in a business, such as people, intellectual property, equipment, facilities, and even other businesses. While obtaining a key person or piece of equipment can have significant impact, the potential impact is generally greater with acquisition of an entire business. A larger investment is required to secure the component, but greater potential is inherent for enhancement of business performance. For example, while a firm might hire a salesperson to begin selling its core product to a new geographical or end-use market, it might also acquire an entire business to obtain its already established sales organization. If properly conceived the later strategy can get the acquirer's core product into the new market far more quickly than would be likely through an individual hire.

Sometimes a firm <u>must</u> acquire an entire business to obtain the specific asset, resource, or capability needed for effective support of the core business. For example, to obtain a new customer base for its existing products, a firm may need to acquire an entire business already selling to those customers since acquiring only the business' sales organization is not practical, or even possible, at times. Because the acquisition of an entire business has greater impact and is sometimes necessary to obtain the desired component, the following discussion focuses on obtaining business components through acquisition of entire businesses.

As a business progresses from initial definition of its core focus to bridging from the core to adjacent areas of opportunity and, ultimately, to redefinition of its core, there is an ongoing need for effective acquisition of required assets, resources, and capabilities. Therefore, the ability to do effective acquisitions is key to achieving optimization of a business.

Some readers may be familiar with the statistics that began surfacing decades ago regarding the widespread failure of mergers and acquisitions. KPMG, owned by KPMG International, published such studies in both 1999[58] and 2001[59] indicating that most deals either produce no value at all or destroy the value that was present before the combination occurred. While KPMG noted statistical improvement in its second study, the later findings still confirmed that deals largely continued to fail with only 30% producing value. In 2004 Bain & Company published a study which supported the earlier findings of KPMG. Bain found that only 28% of such deals produced significant value. It is important to note that these studies may not be precisely relevant to all genres of acquisitions worldwide. The research focused on large, high-impact transactions between large public companies rather than smaller, less diversified and less complex deals.

Even so, the reasons for failure as identified by these studies are not altogether mitigated by less size or complexity. More importantly, their findings can help us determine best practices and meticulously apply them. Experience suggests that regardless of size or complexity, there is a common lack of knowledge as to the most important factors governing the completion of successful acquisitions. In addition, sometimes an awareness of the key factors exists, yet preventable errors occur. This indicates less than meticulous attention to detail or, in some cases, a lack of discipline.

It is not hard to imagine the loss of wealth the world suffers as a result of ineffective mergers and acquisitions. Even in cases where deals neither create nor destroy value, we have still wasted valuable opportunities for timely growth of core businesses. In instances where value is actually destroyed, we have lost not only the opportunities for growth, but also some of the value already present before the deals were done.

Given the importance of acquisitions to support pursuit of the core focus throughout the cycle from original definition to eventual redefinition, little, if any doubt remains that the failure of mergers and acquisitions contributes significantly to the general under-optimization of business.

The need for significant improvement in business regarding management of the core focus, timely divestiture of non-core components, and acquisition of components needed to support the core is obvious. Without a doubt, underachievement in these three areas is a significant factor in the present non-optimization of the business sphere.

Underperformance of individual firms is one of the reasons that the business sphere is not positioned to effectively express the WGTSP principle and its associated benefits. In a WGTSP phenomenon, each part is expected to perform competently in its own right, as a basis for interacting effectively with the other parts. If businesses are not achieving their individual optimum potentials, they will not be able to contribute fully to the coordinated interaction that results in achievement of WGTSP benefits. The steps necessary to optimize the performance of individual businesses and to position them to contribute their part to the expression of the WGTSP principle in business will be our next focus.

Bringing the Actual Situation into Alignment with the Ideal

In order to achieve maximum generation of wealth from individual businesses their performance of key business competencies must be upgraded to the optimum level. Generally, the prescription for accomplishing this is the same for each of the categories of competency:

1. We must collectively develop a comprehensive set of "best practices" for each area of competency. Certain parties will be optimally positioned to contribute to this initiative. For example, leading thinkers and researchers who have studied businesses' failures and successes will be able to contribute significantly to the development of the necessary standards for best practice. In addition, important input can come from the business executives with established successful track records in the effective application of one or more of the key competencies. These individuals can be identified as those who had primary responsibility for the relevant pockets of success in the business sphere.

2. Once consensus as to the standards for best practice is established, we must ensure that pertinent business executives receive thorough training in the mastery of these standards. Presently education of business leaders occurs largely on a voluntary basis, in business schools or professional development seminars. Although these programs contribute to the betterment of business, substantial room remains for improvement in the competencies related to identification and management of the business core, timely divestiture of non-core components, and effective acquisition of components to support pursuit of the core. To allow business leaders to pursue a mastery of these very important skill sets on a voluntary basis is to agree to perpetuation of the current non-optimized state. Clearly, mandatory education in the acknowledged best practices, once identified, is in the best interest globally. Executives themselves will experience greater personal satisfaction when their businesses achieve increased success. The education of each pertinent executive should continue until a high level of optimization in the executive's business is certified.

    The educational program should be administered by a formally created organization, empowered to inspire mastery of the key competencies in the shortest time, through awarding achievement incentives and penalizing underachievement for both individual executives and their businesses. Rather than create an external body to administer the program, a specially formed department within the relevant industry trade association should be responsible, since they are intimately familiar with the issues within their industry segments. Any segment that does not have a specifically defined trade association should form a new body made up of individuals from that sector to be responsible for promoting maximum competence. With this approach, the industry segment can be responsible for achieving its own higher levels of optimization rather than having this initiative administered from outside of their industry. The industry group may ultimately need to have accountability to an authority outside of their business sphere, but only in the broadest sense. More micro-level details should be left to those having a personal stake and greater relevant experience and understanding. Appendix A contains additional comments on the mastery of the three individual business core competencies.

Optimized Performance of Individual Firms, but Not Enough Added Wealth

Before moving on, it should be noted that merely optimizing the performance of individual firm key competencies will not by itself produce the magnitude of additional wealth required to address our serious socio-ecological difficulties.

While mastery of best practices by pertinent business executives will do much to strengthen the performance of key business competencies, it will not likely generate the magnitude of additional wealth that world problems will demand. Surprisingly, in particularly large mature markets, especially during tighter economic conditions, improved individual business performance merely shifts wealth from the losers to the winners. This does little to increase the overall wealth of the industry segment of the firms. Substantial increased wealth of the overall segment can only occur to the extent that a mastery of business practices increases the market-wide volume of sales or reduces costs for the suppliers to those markets. These pivotal ideas are illustrated in the following figure 3.

Costs of supplying the segment's customers   **Wealth created by the firms supplying the market**

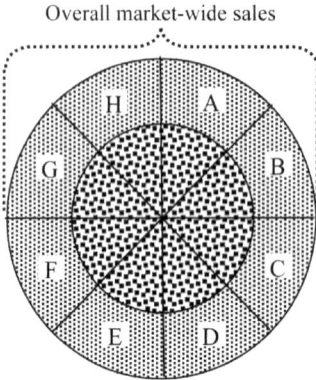

Overall market-wide sales — Each firm (A-G) has a share of the overall market

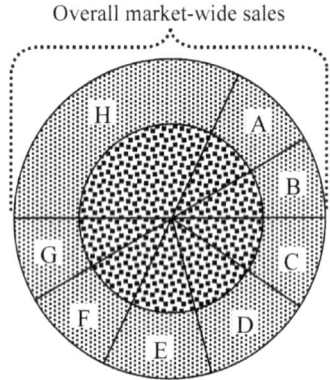

Because overall market size grows slowly, the sales gain of one firm merely shifts wealth from the losers (A-G) to the winner (H), but does not increase the magnitude of wealth of the overall market.

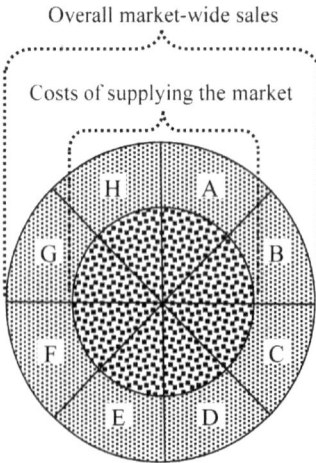

Generated segment wealth = overall market sales minus costs of supplying the market

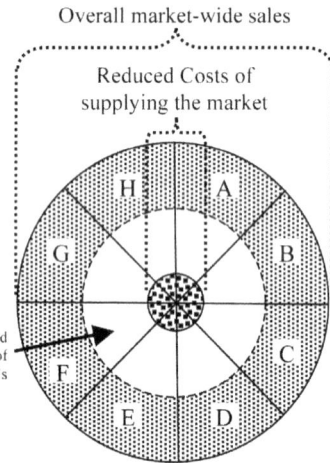

With a slow growing overall market size, the only way to significantly increase the overall segment wealth is to reduce the costs of supplying the market.

Added wealth generated by reducing the costs of supplying the segment's customers

Figure 3.

Improvements in performance of individual firm competencies can only lead to increased overall market sizes if customer demand supports the increased sales. In the larger, more mature markets of the world, like North America and Western Europe, overall growth is slow even during times of general economic growth. In the recent economic contraction, customer demand has been reduced by decreased disposable wealth, slowing the growth of all but the most robust developing markets of the world.

Of course, there are exceptions to this general view, but it still remains that the ongoing global economic difficulties have severely diminished our ability to increase market sizes.

The reduction of costs required to supply the market is an alternative means of increasing overall segment wealth. An individual firm could become more efficient and cost effective by mastering business performance. However, in a competitive arena, the advantaged firm will be hesitant to share its superior abilities with its competitors and thereby give up its advantage. Additionally, maintaining market position requires firms to not cut costs so deeply, as to weaken competitive standing. Therefore, it is unlikely that in our competitive model reduction of costs can be counted as a significant way for an industry segment to increase its overall wealth.

Even if we master best practices in acquisitions and divestitures, and learn how to do transactions that create rather than destroy value[60], the presently reduced volume of deals is likely to limit the resulting gain. Also under our current approach, individual firms will not be likely to allocate significant portions of their performance gains to funding of solutions to the world's serious problems. They did not contribute at the required level even before our present global economic malaise.[61] It may take a significant period of resumed growth before even the former level of philanthropic activity is restored.

Mastery of individual business performance is an important first step toward allowing the business sphere to express the WGTSP principle. But optimization of individual firm performance will not by itself result in the magnitude of additional wealth required to address the world's serious challenges. We must look to full expression of the WGTSP effect to generate the necessary funds to address the serious challenges before us. This leads us to the discussion in Chapter Three of the second issue that hinders application of the WGTSP principle within the global business sphere.

Chapter Three
Individual Businesses as the Parts of a Greater Whole

The business sphere is at the core of the world's economic capability. Our current approach to business is chiefly responsible for the present economic output that is under-achieving its potential by many trillions of dollars annually. Presented below is the second factor that prevents expression of the WGTSP principle by the global business sphere:

> The competitive dynamics that currently dominate inter-firm functioning within each industry segment prevent individual firms from comfortably participating in the kinds of communication and interaction that would allow them to produce the greater whole, the much needed vast additional wealth that would result from application of the WGTSP principle. The business sphere's competitive dynamics not only deprive us of the greater whole (1 + 1 = greater than 2), but also incur costs to each firm of trying to thwart the success of its competitors. This reduces each firm's wealth even more because of the distractive effects of competition (1 + 1 = less than 2).

Currently, the world's industry segments lack the dynamic essential for the success of any group working toward a common objective. Such a dynamic is present in the following examples. The success of an athletic team requires that each player knows his/her role and that all positions work together to achieve victory. The building of a house requires that carpenters, plumbers, electricians and multiple other trades-people each become synchronized with the architect's blueprint, and then work together to complete the finished home within the specified timeline and budget. Even at the micro-level of business, coordination and cooperation exists within each firm as its assets, resources, and capabilities are aligned and harnessed together toward achievement of the firm's agreed upon mission.

However, minimal effort is made to achieve macro-level optimization of the overall industry segment within which the individual firms operate. This point is illustrated in Figure 4. An industry segment is defined as a business environment in which firms are competing for orders from the same group of customers.

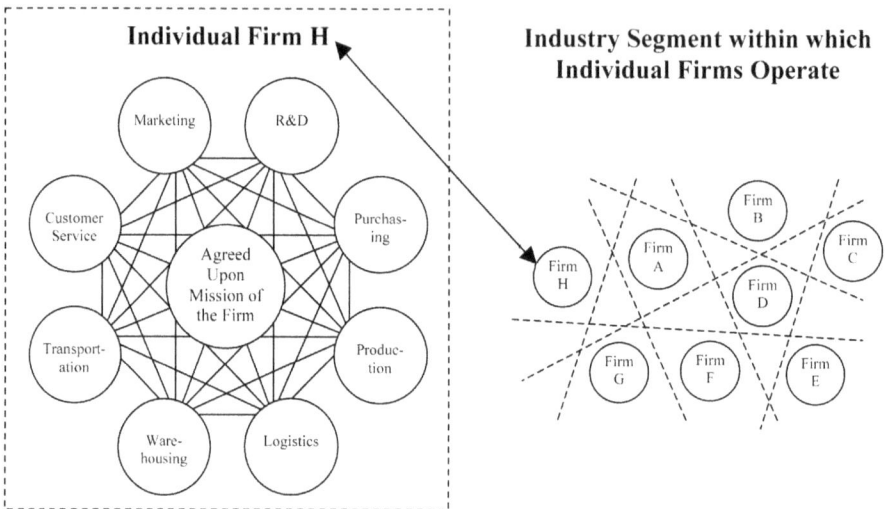

The departments of an individual firm align themselves with the overall agreed upon mission and work together in order to optimize the wealth-generative capacity of the business.

Despite the obvious importance of teamwork in individual firms, minimal coordination and cooperation exists among the firms in each of the world's industry segments. As a result, the full wealth-generative potential of each segment goes unrealized.

Figure 4.

The firms within each segment are, at best, uncoordinated and non-co-operative, and at worst, actively working to block one another's achievements. While we generally pay lip service to the desirability of win/win outcomes, each industry segment is permeated with an inter-firm win/lose dynamic. We are so used to this paradigm of business that we may not immediately see the issue. Imagine an individual firm with no mission around which to rally, no coordination of the firm's assets, resources, and capabilities, and no desire to advance the initiatives of the other departments. This nightmare of dysfunction would be the ultimate model of poor business management. Clearly, such a firm would severely compromise its ability to achieve its full potential. Yet this situation within an individual firm is analogous to what we are suffering at a more macro level within each industry segment. Unfortunately, we are so used to the situation that we do not recognize it for the problem it really is. Or perhaps we do not understand that an industry segment can generate wealth that is greater than the mere stand-alone results of its individual firms. Or as Chapter Eleven will consider, maybe a deeper psychological reason moves us to adopt a business approach that so severely underperforms the wealth-generative potential of the global business sphere.

Analogous to an individual firm, an industry segment has a wealth-generative capacity that can be realized only if all of its components (the segment's firms) are coordinated around an overall mission and are harnessed into the achievement of that mission. Figure 5 below illustrates the contrast between a typical present-day industry segment and the more coordinated

Typical Industry Segment Lacking Coordination and Cooperation

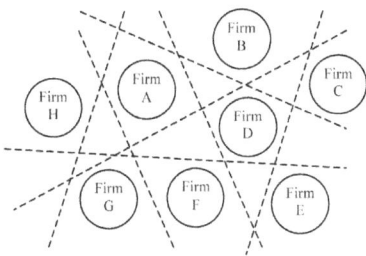

Industry Segment Infused with Coordination and Cooperation

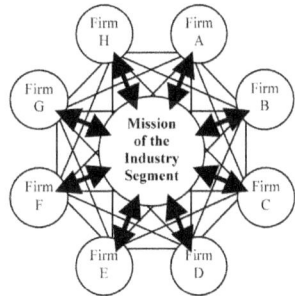

There is minimal coordination and cooperation amongst firms. Rather, the firms pursue their own interests and even battle one another.

Through alignment with the segment-wide mission and cooperation with one another, firms would be able to achieve a result greater than the mere sum of their individual efforts and realize the full wealth-generative potential of the industry segment.

Figure 5.

and cooperative WGTSP ideal that could generate vast additional wealth while promoting maximum balance and harmony.

Far from the ideal shown above, the firms in each industry segment are predominantly self-interested and battle with one another. As a result, each segment's overall potential goes unrealized, many trillions of dollars are squandered annually, and we become more deeply immersed in the economic and socio-ecological problems that are likely to escalate dramatically, becoming tragically irreversible at some point in time.[62]

Pursuing Alignment with the WGTSP Principle

How, specifically, can infusing coordination and cooperation into the world's industry segments generate vast additional wealth? To answer this question, we must look deeply into how the whole can be greater than the mere sum of its parts within an industry segment.

In typical present-day industry segments, individual firms pursue their own interests and refrain from inter-firm coordination and cooperation. This is once again illustrated in Figure 6 below.

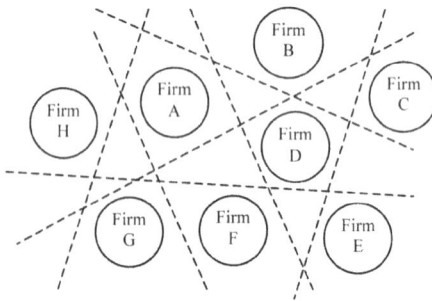

Figure 6.

In this situation, each firm works toward achievement of its goals, but gives little attention to creating a greater whole through constructive interaction among firms. Without constructive inter-firm interaction, nothing additional beyond the stand-alone activities of the individual firms in the segment is created. However, if the firms coordinate and cooperate, a whole that exceeds their stand-alone results is possible.

Each of the diagrams shown in Figure 7 represents an industry segment having coordination and cooperation. In each of the diagrams, lines are drawn between all of the firms. The lines represent possible avenues of constructive interaction from firm to firm. Figure 7 clearly demonstrates that as the number of firms in an industry segment increases, so does the number of possible channels of coordination and cooperation. The examples shown depict theoretical segments containing three, four, five, six, and eight firms. The three-firm segment contains the possibility of three lines of interaction, while twenty-seven lines of interaction are possible in the segment containing eight firms.

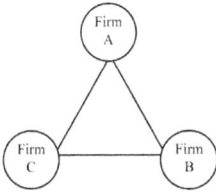

An industry segment with 3 firms, has 3 possible lines of constructive interaction.

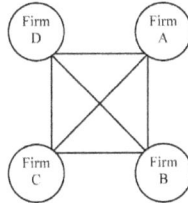

An industry segment with 4 firms, has 6 possible lines of constructive interaction.

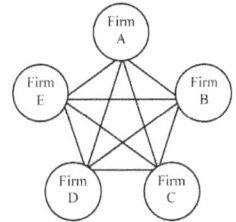

An industry segment with 5 firms, has 10 possible lines of constructive interaction.

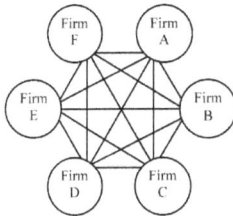

An industry segment with 6 firms, has 14 possible lines of constructive interaction.

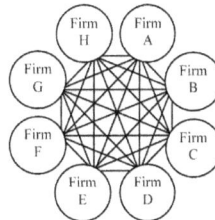

An industry segment with 8 firms, has 28 possible lines of constructive interaction.

Figure 7.

Each line in the segments shown above symbolizes the possibility of constructive interaction between two firms, but Figure 8, reveals the potential for pursuit of multiple forms of cooperation along each line.

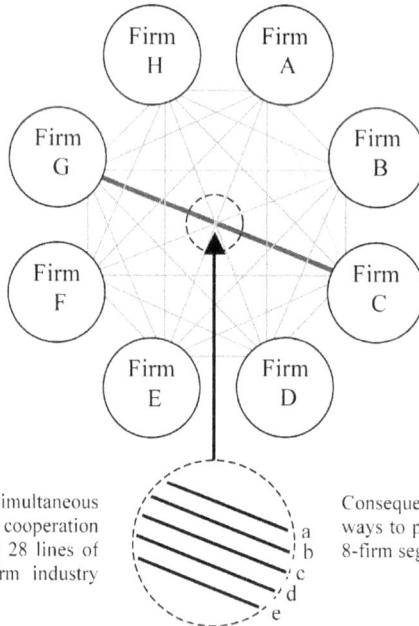

There is the potential for simultaneous pursuit of multiple forms of cooperation (a-e, etc.) along each of the 28 lines of interrelationship in an 8-firm industry segment.

Consequently the number of possible ways to promote cooperation within an 8-firm segment is many multiples of 28

Figure 8.

Most real-world industry segments contain much more than eight significant firms, often 35 or more. A segment containing 35 firms has 560 possible lines of constructive interaction. While many types of cooperation exist, we will examine just five of the most common categories. Considering just five categories, offers as many as 2800 (560 X 5 = 2800) separate collaborative initiatives in a 35 firm industry segment.

This number represents enormous potential for creation of additional wealth beyond what is currently forthcoming from our global industrial sphere. Detailed review of the five common types of collaboration illustrate specifically how infusion of coordination and cooperation in the world's industry segments will lead to creation of vast additional wealth, a whole much greater than the sum of its parts. These five types of collaboration are broadly known and understood in the public domain, and are powerful ways of reducing costs and increasing efficiencies, thereby generating additional wealth without any increase in segment-wide market size or revenues.

Five Common Types of Collaboration

Five types of effective collaboration include:

- Sharing of support functions needed by all firms
- Optimization of production assets
- Segment-wide sharing of know-how
- Optimization of selling assets
- Centralized purchasing of raw materials and supplies

Sharing of Support Functions Needed by All Firms

Typical kinds of support functions are used by each firm in an industry segment. Any firm lacking such support is at a serious competitive disadvantage to the point of losing its market position. Because minimal coordination and cooperation are currently practiced within the world's existing industry segments, each firm is obliged to maintain its own support functions, separate from those of every other firm. This creates enormous redundancy that is both wasteful and a barrier to the transmission of know-how and the adoption of best practices across the segment.

Consider this closer examination of the waste incurred by this redundancy. Typical support functions used by each firm in an industry segment might include research and development (R&D), marketing, strategic planning, engineering, maintenance, sales and distribution, purchasing, logistics, warehousing, shipping/ transportation, customer service, technical support, quality assurance, safety, environmental compliance, information technology, human resources (HR), accounting, administration, etc. No aspect of most of these functions needs to be fully dedicated to any one particular firm. Aspects of some functions may need to be single firm-dedicated, but not all. For example, each firm may need a dedicated quality assurance inspector, but quality planning and administration need not be the exclusive resource of an individual firm. With minor exceptions, the support functions that each firm currently maintains separately can be centralized within an industry segment to provide support to all of the segment's firms. An enormous reduction of overhead costs within each firm would result while maintaining revenues. Consequently, vast additional wealth would be generated. To further appreciate the magnitude of this opportunity, consider the following hypothetical example of typical individual firm overhead categories and corresponding estimated annual costs.

$ 7 million – R&D
  4 million – Marketing
  2 million – Strategic planning
  2 million – Engineering
  1 million – Maintenance
  6 million – Sales and distribution
  2 million – Purchasing
  1 million – Logistics
  3 million – Warehousing
  2 million – Shipping/ transportation
  1 million – Customer service
  2 million – Technical support
  2 million – Quality assurance
  1 million – Safety
  1 million – Environmental compliance
  2 million – Information technology
  3 million – Human resources (HR)
  2 million – Accounting
  3 million – Administration

This individual firm would spend approximately $ 47 million annually in hopes of remaining competitive and retaining market position. If this were the average annual per-firm spending within our typical 35 firm industry segment, the aggregate annual costs of the segment would be $ 1.65 billion. Of course, some firms in the segment would spend more and some less, but the point is still made that substantial annual costs will be incurred if each firm continues to maintain its own dedicated support functions. Considering that North America alone, has around 1200 significant industry segments[63],

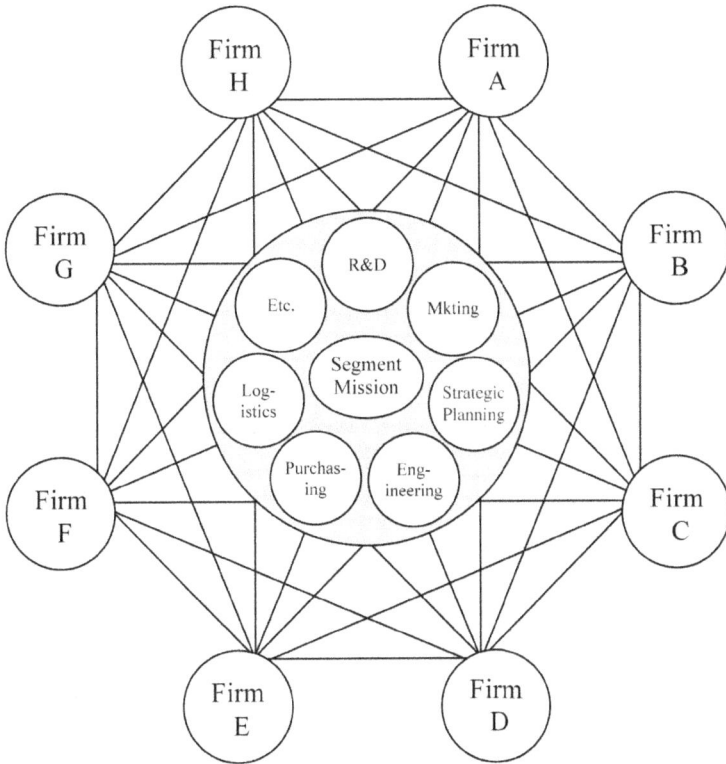

Through coordination and cooperation within an industry segment, support functions can be centralized and shared among segment firms. So long as diseconomies of scale are avoided, redundancies would be eliminated and costs vastly reduced, while maintaining segment-wide sales.

Figure 9.

the wealth consumed by the <u>global</u> industrial sphere to maintain duplicated support functions is, no doubt, several trillions of dollars annually.

Creating centralized support functions that serve the needs of <u>all</u> firms in a segment, instead of just one can eliminate a substantial amount of cost. Caution should be exercised to determine the mass required of each centralized function so that in the pursuit of reduced costs, no diseconomies of scale[64] are created that deprive individual firms of the magnitude, quality, or timeliness of support they need to effectively achieve their business objectives. But without a doubt, eliminating the support function redundancies presently existing in the world's many industry segments would remove massive costs.

Optimization of Production Assets

Each firm that produces a product or renders a service possesses the means to do so. Typically products are produced in facilities and services are rendered by organizations. Depending on the firm's volume of sales, the facilities may be fully utilized or underutilized. Underutilized facilities or organizations logically produce less wealth. Conversely, fully utilized facilities and organizations produce more wealth, but may also suffer some lost opportunities for customer orders due to lack of available production capacity. In this case, as well as in underutilization, the lack of coordination and cooperation among the firms in an industry segment can obstruct the gain of segment-wide wealth.

How can this be so? A 35 firm segment will generally have many firms with underutilized facilities and organizations, and/or occasions of customer

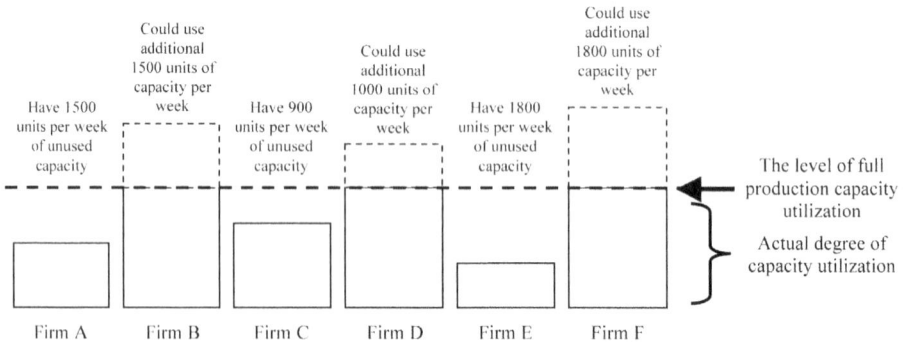

In the hypothetical case shown above Firms A, C, and E collectively have unused capacity of 4200 units per week, that negatively impacts the profitability of each firm. Due to their limited capacity, firms B, D, and F collectively have un-pursued customer orders of 4200 units per week which, if pursued, could substantially enhance the wealth of each firm. Without inter-firm coordination and cooperation, all six firms experience loss. But with coordination and cooperation, available capacity in the segment can be used to produce the segment's un-pursued sales. As a result, the wealth-generative capacity of the segment can be optimized and all individual firms benefited.

Figure 10.

orders lost due to lack of available production capacity. Without inter-firm coordination and cooperation, any firm suffering from either of these two conditions has a problem that cannot be quickly or cheaply remedied. But, if all 35 firms communicate with one another about their shortage of orders or the capacity to produce orders, they will probably discover ways they could cooperate so as to maximize both utilization and sales. Such initiatives will help optimize the wealth-generative capacity of the industry segment, but this can only happen with inter-firm coordination and cooperation.

Segment-Wide Sharing of Know-How

Individual firms sometimes possess or develop superior know-how giving them a competitive advantage over other firms in the industry segment. Such know-how may bring great advantage to the owner by decreasing costs, improving efficiencies, or increasing sales for the firm. Sharing this know-how with the other firms in the segment would reduce the owner's competitive advantage, yet sharing the know-how could greatly increase the wealth of the segment at large.

For example, an individual firm may develop a new process which significantly reduces the production costs. As a result, it may substantially improve its profits. However, if this know-how were shared throughout the segment, every firm would achieve an increase in profitability and optimize the wealth generative capacity of the segment as a whole. Only with a cooperative attitude are the special capabilities of individual firms likely to produce segment-wide optimization of wealth.

The unrestricted sharing of know-how can not only optimize the wealth-generative potential of the overall industry segment, but also effectively spread consumer-benefiting product innovations and technologies that promote ecological sustainability. So, segment-wide cooperation can both maximize the generation of wealth and promote most effectively the interests of society.

Optimization of Selling Assets

Firms that provide a product or service utilize some means to sell their offering to the relevant customer base. Especially with end-use or geographical markets that are growing, some portions of the relevant customer bases may remain unaddressed because the selling effort is not fully developed, as when sales forces or distributors are too sparsely positioned to achieve optimum contact with potential customers.

Even though any one business may lack the selling resources necessary to reach all of its potential customers, other providers of non-competing products and services, may possess underutilized sales forces or distributors needed by the businesses with under-optimized sales. Coordination and collaboration among such businesses could allow the under-penetrated business to achieve maximum sales presence in a much shorter time, while increasing profits by making fuller use of the otherwise under-utilized selling assets of the more fully developed businesses. As a result, the short falls being experienced by all parties would be transformed into greater wealth for all participants.

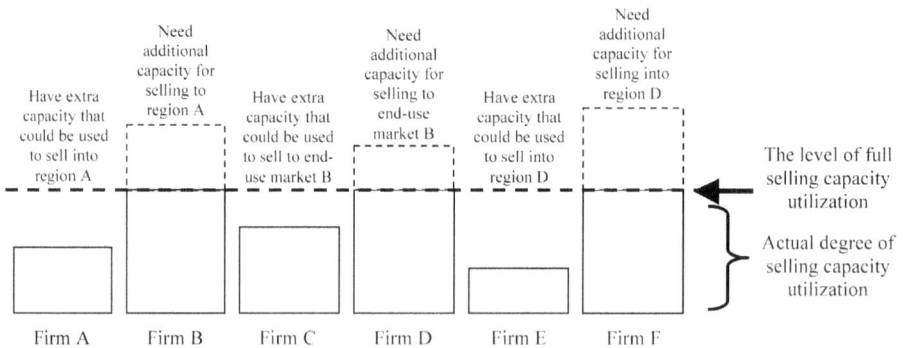

In the hypothetical case shown above, Firms A, C, and E collectively have unused selling capacity that under-optimizes the profitability of each firm. Due to their limited selling capacity, firms B, D, and F collectively have under-optimized penetration of their respective potential customer bases that, if pursued, could substantially enhance the wealth of each firm. Without inter-firm coordination and cooperation, all six firms experience loss. But through coordination and cooperation, available selling capacity in the segment can be used to reach the unaddressed customer bases. As a result, the wealth-generative capacity of the segment can be optimized and all individual firms benefited.

Figure 11.

Volume Purchasing of Raw Materials and Supplies

Firms can generally pay lower prices per unit by purchasing larger volumes of raw materials and supplies resulting in substantial cost savings for a firm. Firms usually place their supply and material orders separately. In some instances firms will place group orders for the very purpose of receiving better unit prices, but this is the exception rather than the rule. As a result, many firms in each industry segment pay higher unit prices and thus hinder the generation of wealth. Through segment-wide coordination and collaboration, group purchasing would be the norm and thus reduce each firm's related costs and optimize the wealth-generative capacity of the segment as a whole.

But will the supplier base be negatively impacted if their customers pay less per unit? If the wealth-generative potential of the supplier base gets reduced by their customer's gain, a mere shifting of the benefit would result without adding any new wealth in the overall sense. This seems logical, but is not necessarily the case.

Wealth will, in fact, be added overall if the supplier base also coordinates and cooperates within itself by employing the five categories of collaboration discussed earlier. As a result, the supplier base will also experience reduced costs and improved efficiencies. In fact, introduction of coordination and cooperation in an industry segment should both encourage and support collaboration within each other industry segment throughout the value chain. This point is illustrated in Figure 12.

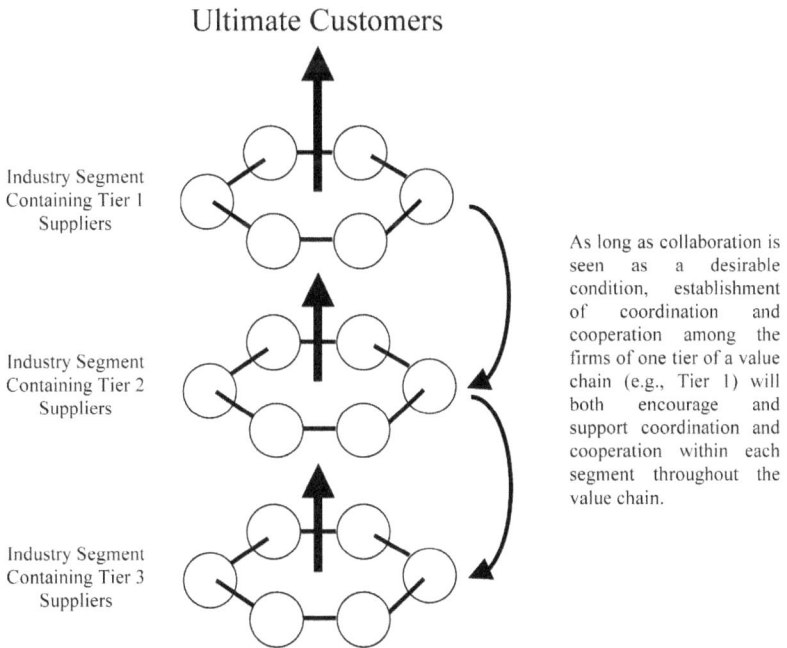

As long as collaboration is seen as a desirable condition, establishment of coordination and cooperation among the firms of one tier of a value chain (e.g., Tier 1) will both encourage and support coordination and cooperation within each segment throughout the value chain.

Figure 12.

The Power of Coordination and Cooperation in the Business Sphere

This chapter has explained how the lack of teamwork in the world's many industry segments is enormously wasteful. Five common categories of collaboration have been presented that should be applied to global business in order to generate the vast additional wealth that will be needed to solve the world's serious problems. Several trillion dollars of additional wealth could be generated annually by the first of the five categories alone. What follows is evidence that the inter-firm collaboration being proposed will actually succeed in generating the desired additional wealth.

Evidence that Inter-firm Coordination and Cooperation will Work

Evidence of the effectiveness of collaboration within the business sphere can be found in three circumstances. The first occurred during the era of trusts and monopolies in the late 1800s and early 1900s in America.[65] During this time large numbers of businesses held under common ownership collaborated both horizontally and vertically to produce powerful operational and market efficiencies.[66] These enhanced efficiencies allowed the collaborators to profitably lower prices enough to drive competitors out of business, therefore bestowing monopoly status on the survivors. The monopolies then raised prices and lowered wages in an attempt to further concentrate their wealth and financial power. The disregard for the common good demonstrated by these trusts and monopolies eventually lead to the enactment of laws prohibiting such unbridled business practices.[67] While the selfish abuses by the trusts and monopolies cannot be condoned, they do illustrate the economic effectiveness of inter-firm coordination and collaboration. Unlike the trusts, GEO will infuse an even greater degree of cooperation and then harness this wealth-generative power for the common good rather than the interests of a privileged few.

Secondly the present day phenomenon of mergers and acquisitions also demonstrates the effectiveness of inter-firm coordination and collaboration. In M&A, one business buys another or the two businesses merge their assets so that they can coordinate strategies and pursue specific forms of cooperation. Historically, 70% to 80% of such transactions have not created the additional wealth as intended.[68] This lamentable deficiency has arisen due to carelessness, disregard of pertinent transaction-specific information, and a general lack of deep understanding regarding the factors that govern the success or failure of such initiatives.

Chapter Two calls for the development and uniform application of best practices regarding mergers and acquisitions. Widespread use of such best practices, along with increased discretion and good judgment, will no doubt reverse M&A's dismal track record and provide a basis to maximize related wealth generation.[69] Under our present approach, additional wealth accrues to the immediate stakeholders of the businesses involved and merely trickles down to society at large. Through GEO, the additional wealth will directly benefit society at large, in addition to generating for participating firms higher earnings than they make now using their present approach to business.

Most importantly, while the majority of mergers and acquisitions do not currently produce the intended result, those that are properly executed, concretely confirm the potential for generating increased wealth through inter-firm coordination and collaboration. In fact, the current successful portion of M&A activity has contributed significantly in recent decades to globalization and the creation of multi-national corporations[70] that have the ability to increase their wealth and influence thanks to the powers of coordination and collaboration.[71]

The third circumstance that speaks to the effectiveness of inter-firm coordination and cooperation is the common use in business of joint ventures, strategic alliances, and numerous other forms of collaboration. Such practices do not necessarily result in one business being owned by another, as is the case in acquisitions, but they can create extra wealth for the participants who are often arch rivals in other respects. Industry offers many examples of cooperative initiatives, for example:

Collaborative Buying Separate firms sometimes achieve economies of scale and increased efficiencies by combining their efforts in the purchasing of raw materials or supplies.

Consider the following:

- Competing automakers Daimler and BMW pool their efforts in the purchasing of mechanical systems, wheels, and tires. BMW claims that the co-purchasing arrangement is applied to 10% of completed car components, without any damage to the competitor's respective brands. The collaboration is expected to save BMW four billion euros of costs in 2012.[72]

- PepsiCo and Anheuser-Busch have agreed to a collaborative purchasing agreement in which information technology, office supplies, travel and facilities management, and office maintenance are co-purchased.[73] The collaboration is expected to create significant efficiencies and cost savings.

- Hundreds of small businesses in Boston, Massachusetts have teamed together to co-purchase electricity from Constellation New Energy. These small businesses have collectively agreed to buy 117,000,000 kilowatt-hours of electricity guaranteed at lower fixed prices for a year.[74]

Collaborative Marketing and Distribution   Individual firms may market and distribute their products cooperatively to save costs and/or more comprehensively penetrate their addressable markets. Such is the case in the following specific examples:

- By pooling their selling efforts outside North America, the consortium of Saskatchewan potash fertilizer producers comprised of Agrium Inc, The Mosaic Company, and Potash Corporation of Saskatchewan Inc, operates as the world's largest exporter of potash. Known as Canpotex, the group sells 8-9 million metric tons of potash annually, and supplies major markets in Australia, Brazil, China, India, Indonesia, Japan, Korea, and Malaysia.[75]

- The four major cotton marketing cooperatives in the U.S. collectively export half of the nation's cotton to the world's textile mills. The overarching consortium known as AMCOT represents the collective interests of its cotton-growing member co-ops, Calcot, Plains Cotton Cooperative Association, Carolinas Cotton Growers Cooperative, and Staplcotn.[76]

Collaborative Technical Development   Sometimes separate firms with complementary technical competencies can team together to achieve engineering and/or manufacturing-related advances. Some examples follow:

- BlueScope Steel of Australia and Nippon Steel of Japan have collaborated to develop the industry's next generation coated steel

> for use in the building and construction markets. The new product
> is expected to offer superior corrosion resistance as well as an
> improved environmental profile.[77]

- To extend its sales base, Sharp Corporation of Japan licensed
  its know-how to Utstarcom Inc. of California in the USA to
  manufacture and sell electronic products from Utstarcom's
  subsidiary in Peoples' Republic of China.[78]

- Gulf Air Conditioning Manufacturing Industries, LLC entered
  into collaboration with Hitachi Air Conditioning Systems Co.
  Ltd. of Japan to produce chilled water air conditioning equipment
  and distribute Japanese quality air conditioning systems to the
  region. The agreement allows Hitachi to establish sales bases in the
  Middle Eastern and North African markets.[79]

Collaborative Logistics and Transportation   Separate firms can band together to enhance the efficiency of their collective efforts in logistics and
transportation. Cost savings for producers as well as increased customer
service was achieved in the case of Zoetwaren Distributie Nederland (ZDN:
Dutch Sweets Distribution), a group of eight competing medium-sized
Dutch sweets and candy producers. Prior to the collaboration each of the
eight competitors delivered separately to the same 250 drop-off points, but
in 1993 the costs of each producer were decreased by combining and coordinating their collective logistics and transportation efforts.[80]

    The foregoing is a small sampling of the variety of business collabora-
tions that exist in the world. All such arrangements demonstrate the effectiveness of inter-firm coordination and cooperation to produce additional
wealth beyond what can be achieved without collaborative interaction.

Regulatory Barriers to Inter-firm Coordination and Cooperation

Given the proven effectiveness of inter-firm coordination and cooperation,
it is surprising that collaboration is not more pervasive in the world's industry segments. Even though the potential benefits seem compelling, especially during this time of economic difficulty and looming socio-ecological

problems, legislation continues to deter full-blown inter-firm coordination and collaboration.

Legal statutes in many jurisdictions of the world closely scrutinize and, in some cases, might even prevent the kind of cooperation envisioned in GEO.[81] Such laws were created to protect customers and competitors from the kind of damage that occurred when unregulated firms (monopolies) pursued powerful business efficiencies and the resulting wealth maximization, but failed to appropriately distribute the profits to the general good.

But these abuses happened in a former time and under different circumstances than today. Our current situation demands that we maximize the generation of wealth to effectively address the economic and socio-ecological difficulties we are facing. The global business sphere holds enormous latent potential that can be unlocked through full-blown inter-firm coordination and cooperation within each industry segment. Now is the time to unlock this potential for the common good. We must pursue these achievable gains while mitigating the chances that individual greed will result in abuse by the business sphere. The vast additional wealth which will be created could solve the problems we are facing and make participating firms wealthier. Without redistributing current wealth, GEO can foster the common good through an approach that generates vast additional wealth far beyond what is currently produced by global business.

In order to avoid the abuse that could result from maximized inter-firm collaboration, proper conditions must be established from the start to insure the best use of profits. A bilateral agreement between government and participating businesses will outline these conditions. First, government will adjust the statutes to allow full inter-firm collaboration. In return, businesses will agree that a substantial portion of the generated additional wealth will be used for the common good and that they will submit to necessary levels of transparency and monitoring. With the government's blessings, the business sphere will have the opportunity to take the lead in generating the funds necessary to ensure the world's survival and ongoing progress. Government will have the comfort of knowing that without increasing deficits or taxing present earnings, and without increasing governmental involvement in the private sector, promotion of the common good will be maximized.

Even if business agrees to the above conditions and government adjusts the statutes, one last condition must still be remedied to allow full expression of the WGTSP principle within the business sphere. An explanation follows.

Structural Changes Needed to Support Full Expression of the WGTSP Principle

Chapter One stated that, contrary to the high degree of functional special-ization and coordination found within true expressions of the WGTSP prin-ciple, the business sphere fosters tremendous duplication of efforts while firms within the same industry segment actively try to usurp one another's roles and resources, and even obstruct one another's success. This condition not only suppresses the benefits of the WGTSP principle, but also fosters inter-firm mistrust, making it even more difficult for firms to engage in the collaborative efforts necessary to achieve the full wealth-generative poten-tials of their respective industry segments. We simply cannot afford any practices that deprive us of the funds needed to address our economic mal-aise and the rapidly approaching socio-ecological difficulties. Businesses absolutely must work together as a cohesive and cooperative team.

Clearly, we must infuse coordination and collaboration into the global business sphere, but it cannot easily happen under present circumstances. Our culture has long believed in the win/loss model, so we have constructed a global business sphere that is aligned with the same dynamics. Under present conditions, firms within an industry segment do not feel naturally inclined to cooperate with one another. In many instances, they are battling each oth-er for customer orders, so cooperation would amount to "aiding and abet-ting the enemy." In fact, responsibility to the stakeholders necessitates that each firm does everything possible to "win", which, of course, means that the competitor must lose. Without changing this dynamic where most pro-nounced there is little reason to expect that firms will cooperate and optimize the wealth-generative capacity of the overall industry segment. We must ad-just the situation so that individual firms can feel comfortable functioning as team members rather than combatants. Before we can fully apply the five common categories of collaboration to the global business sphere, we must first eliminate at least the strongest instances of win/loss dynamics, inter-firm duplication of efforts, and usurping of resources. To do this individual firms must adjust the way they do business.

Two Ways of Undoing the Win, Loss Dynamics of the Global Business Sphere

The focus of a segment's firms can be adjusted in two ways so that one firm's win is not another firm's loss:

- Ensure that arch competitors do not sell the same product to the same customer.

- If selling the same product to the same customer is unavoidable, channel each firm's focus into either production or sales/distribution.

Ensure That Arch Competitors Do Not Sell the Same Product to the Same Customer

When multiple firms sell the same product to the same customer, the gain of one firm automatically results in loss for the others. The win/loss dynamics of this situation discourages firms from coordinating their efforts and cooperating, to reduce costs and increase wealth for the industry segment as a whole. The winning firm tries hard to maintain its lead and the losing firms try equally hard to recoup their losses. In doing so, firms attempt to maintain or even increase spending on R&D, training, advertising, etc. The net result is under-achievement of the wealth-generative potential of the segment.

The focus of the firms in a segment can be redirected in six ways to eliminate the win/loss dynamics related to firms selling the same product to the same customer:

Firms in the segment sell altogether different products   An industry segment often has a range of related but non-competing products. For example, in the automotive industry passenger cars, sport utility vehicles, and light trucks are all private-use vehicles, yet each possesses unique functionality. In the first way of eliminating the win/loss dynamics in the segment, each firm focuses on supplying one of its segment's products. Figure 13 illustrates this adjustment. A simple three-firm segment is shown to make the example easier to understand.

The adjustment illustrated requires the manufacturing capacity of each firm to be interchangeable as to product category. For example, if Firm A was previously manufacturing products 1, 2, and 3, but transitions to manufacturing only product 1 at a much increased volume, the capacity previously used for products 2 and 3 must be easily adaptable to product 1.

Adjustment #1 - Needed to eliminate win/loss dynamics

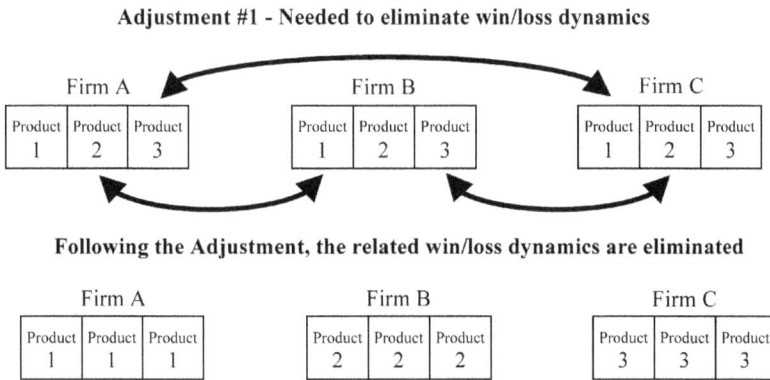

Firm A   Firm B   Firm C

Product 1	Product 2	Product 3

Product 1	Product 2	Product 3

Product 1	Product 2	Product 3

Following the Adjustment, the related win/loss dynamics are eliminated

Firm A   Firm B   Firm C

Product 1	Product 1	Product 1

Product 2	Product 2	Product 2

Product 3	Product 3	Product 3

Figure 13.

In cases where manufacturing capacity is not interchangeable the firms can eliminate the win/ loss dynamics by trading equipment or facilities, or by executing a cooperative agreement. For example, Firm B may agree to pay Firm A to produce product 2 on its behalf.

Firms in the segment sell the same products, but at different price points   Within an industry segment the same product is often sold at non-competing price points. For example, the passenger cars category of the automotive industry has luxury cars, economy cars, and those costing somewhere in between. In the second way of eliminating the win/loss dynamics in the segment, firms concentrate on supplying the same product at one or another of the price points. Figure 14, on following page, illustrates this adjustment. Again, a simple three-firm segment is shown to make the example easier to understand.

The adjustment illustrated requires the manufacturing capacity of each firm to be interchangeable as to product price point. For example, if Firm A was previously manufacturing a product at all price points, but transitions to manufacturing only at the lowest price point at an increased volume, the previous capacity for producing at the medium and highest price points must easily adapt to the lowest. In cases where manufacturing capacity is not interchangeable the firms can trade equipment or facilities, or execute a cooperative agreement in order to eliminate the win/loss dynamics. In other words Firm B may agree to pay Firm A to produce mid-priced product on its behalf.

Adjustment #2 - Needed to eliminate win/loss dynamics

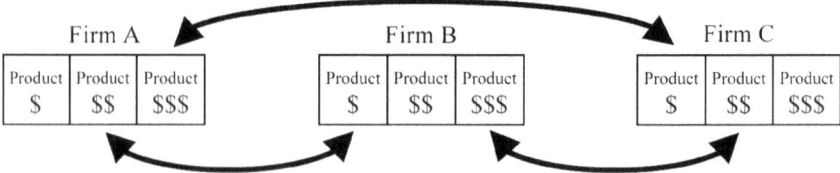

Firm A				Firm B				Firm C		
Product	Product	Product		Product	Product	Product		Product	Product	Product
$	$$	$$$		$	$$	$$$		$	$$	$$$

Following the adjustment, the related win/loss dynamics are eliminated.

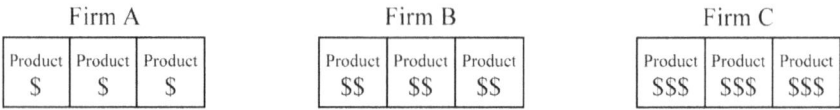

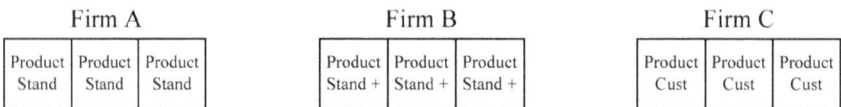

Firm A				Firm B				Firm C		
Product	Product	Product		Product	Product	Product		Product	Product	Product
$	$	$		$$	$$	$$		$$$	$$$	$$$

Figure 14.

Firms in the segment sell either the purely standard, standard with options, or purely custom version of the same product   An industry segment often offers the same product with varying degrees of product options. For example, in the housing industry, homes are sold as standard with very limited options, standard but with some options like fireplaces or skylights, or fully custom designed. In the third way of eliminating the win/ loss dynamics in the segment, each firm concentrates on supplying only a purely standard or a somehow customized version of the product. Figure 15 illustrates this adjustment. The simple three-firm segment makes the example easier to understand.

Adjustment #3 - needed to eliminate win/loss dynamics

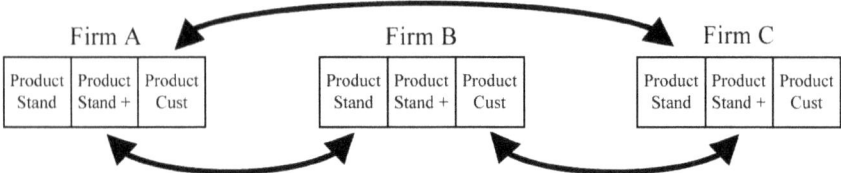

Firm A				Firm B				Firm C		
Product	Product	Product		Product	Product	Product		Product	Product	Product
Stand	Stand +	Cust		Stand	Stand +	Cust		Stand	Stand +	Cust

Following the adjustment, the related win/loss dynamics are eliminated.

Firm A				Firm B				Firm C		
Product	Product	Product		Product	Product	Product		Product	Product	Product
Stand	Stand	Stand		Stand +	Stand +	Stand +		Cust	Cust	Cust

Figure 15.

The adjustment illustrated requires that the manufacturing capacity of each firm be interchangeable as to degree of product customization. For example, if Firm A was previously manufacturing purely standard, somewhat customized, and fully custom products, but transitions to manufacturing only purely standard at an increased volume, the capacity previously used for somewhat customized and fully customized products must easily adapt to purely standard. In cases where manufacturing capacity is not interchangeable, the firms can trade equipment or facilities, or execute a cooperative agreement in order to eliminate the win/loss dynamics. In other words, Firm B can agree to pay Firm A for producing somewhat customized product on its behalf.

Firms in the segment sell the same product into non-overlapping geographical territories within the segment An industry segment may sell the same product to different sets of customers based on varying geographical location. For example, household furnishings are often sold in defined territories, such as the Northeast, Southeast, Southwest, Midwest, etc. In the fourth way of eliminating the win/loss dynamics in the segment, each firm sells to a different geographical territory. Figure 16 illustrates this adjustment. The simple three-firm segment makes the example easier to understand.

Adjustment #4 - needed to eliminate win/loss dynamics

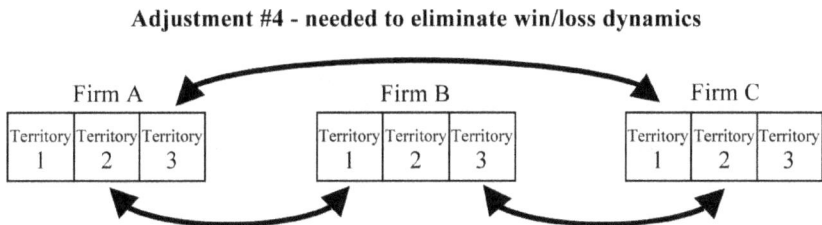

Following the adjustment, the related win/loss dynamics are eliminated.

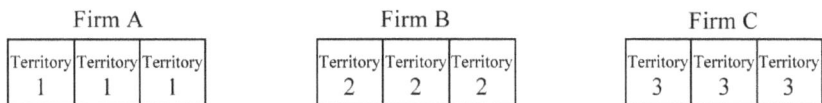

Figure 16.

   The adjustment illustrated relies on the ability of each firm to cover more customer accounts, but within a more focused geographical territory. For example, if Firm A was previously selling in territories 1, 2, and 3, but transitions to supplying only territory 1 at an increased volume, the selling capacity previously used for the expanded range of territories must refocus to cover more accounts in just one territory. In cases where selling capacity cannot refocus, the firms can trade sales personnel and other selling related assets, or execute a cooperative agreement in order to eliminate the win/loss dynamics. In other words Firm B may agree to pay Firm A for selling into territory 2 on its behalf.

Firms in the segment sell the same product to non-overlapping customers based on account size   An industry segment may sell the same product to different sets of customers based on customer account size. For example, office furniture is sold to independent businesses, to regional businesses with multiple branches, and to large, national businesses or governmental agencies. In this fifth way of eliminating the win/loss dynamics in the segment, each firm sells to only customer accounts of small, medium, or large size. Figure 17 illustrates this adjustment, using a simple three-firm segment to make the example easier to understand.

Adjustment #5 - needed to eliminate win/loss dynamics

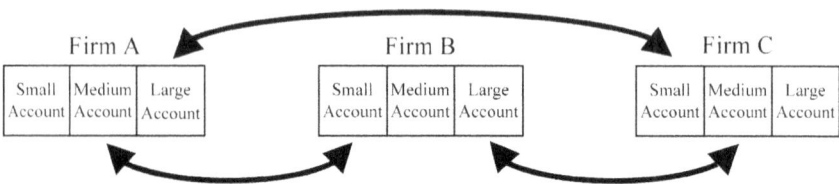

Following the adjustment, the related win/loss dynamics are eliminated.

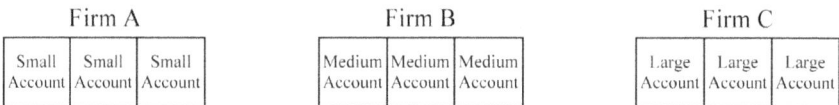

Figure 17.

The adjustment illustrated above relies on each firm's ability to apply the expertise appropriate to the size account it services. For example, if Firm A was previously selling into small, medium, and large-sized accounts, but transitions to supplying only small accounts at an increased volume, the selling capacity previously used for the medium and large-sized accounts must refocus to cover a larger number of small accounts. In cases where selling capacity cannot refocus, the firms can trade sales personnel and other selling related assets, or execute a cooperative agreement in order to eliminate the win/loss dynamics. In other words Firm B may agree to pay Firm A for selling into medium-sized accounts on its behalf.

Firms in the segment sell the same product into non-overlapping end-use markets An industry segment may sell the same product to different sets of customers based on differing end-use markets. For example, the same adhesive or sealant is sold into the marine, aircraft, or automotive markets. In the sixth way of eliminating the win/loss dynamics in the segment, each firm sells to only one end-use market. Figure 18 illustrates this adjustment. Again, a simpler three-firm segment is shown.

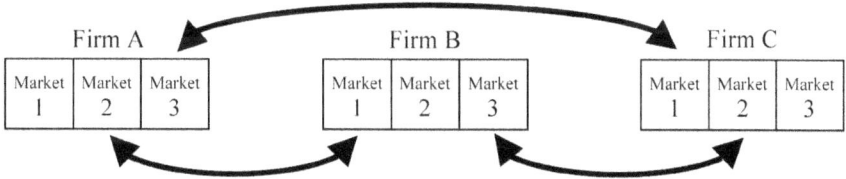

Following the adjustment, the related win/loss dynamics are eliminated.

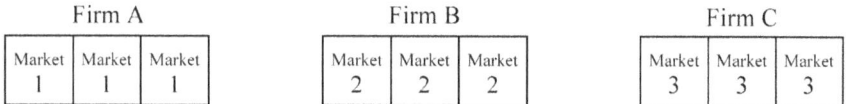

Figure 18.

The adjustment illustrated above relies on each firm to apply the expertise appropriate to the end-use market it services. For example, if Firm A was previously selling into three markets, but transitions to supplying only one market at an increased volume, the selling capacity previously used for the expanded range of markets must refocus to cover more accounts in just one market. In cases where selling capacity is not re-focusable, the firms can trade sales personnel and other selling-related assets, or execute a cooperative agreement in order to eliminate the win/loss dynamics. In other words Firm B may agree to pay Firm A for selling into market 2 on its behalf.

If selling the same product to the same customer cannot be avoided, firms focus on either production or sales/distribution

In cases where firms cannot avoid selling the same product or service to the same customer, the firms can focus on either the production or on the selling/distribution of the orders in question, so as to eliminate the win, loss dynamics. That is, some firms sell/distribute to the customer and provide field support, while other firms manufacture the product. This requires co-ordination and cooperation among the firms involved, but provides a way that manufacturing and selling-focused firms can both benefit from each customer order, rather than a single "winner take all" situation. As with the other six ways of eliminating the win/loss dynamics of an industry segment, such an arrangement clears the way for businesses to infuse the five previously discussed forms of collaboration.

In addition to eliminating the associated win/loss dynamics, GEO allows the business sphere to capitalize on the natural short and long-term advantages enjoyed by the various regions of the world. For example, the U.S. has experienced the migration of several of its industry segments to offshore locations where the costs of production are lower. A nationalistic perspective views this as a sorrowful loss, but a global perspective can view this as a gain because more *overall* wealth is created by lower costs of production. As a result, we can apply more wealth to the world's serious problems than we can through protectionism that discourages businesses from locating in the most cost-advantaged locale. Of course, the added wealth of GEO must be fairly and effectively applied to the problems. Chapter Six will discuss the method for ensuring that the added wealth is properly distributed.

The Win/Win Benefit

Chapter Three has presented structural ways for reversing the win/loss approach that discourages inter-firm coordination and cooperation. Implementation of these remedies will remove the structural basis for the firms that are most concerned about collaboration making them vulnerable to the competitive initiatives of other firms.

But even without full application of these structural remedies, the business sphere should be able to gain interest in the collaboration envisioned in GEO. After all, arch rivals presently collaborate to achieve the wealth-enhancing benefits of initiatives such as collaborative buying, collaborative marketing and distribution, and collaborative logistics and transportation. The key to making such initiatives more prevalent is the creation of an opportunity for firms to derive significant tangible benefit from inter-firm coordination and cooperation. GEO will powerfully accomplish this. Using the GEO formula, wealth generated by the firms' individual efforts will remain with the firms, and the additional wealth generated by inter-firm collaboration will flow into a fund, which will be used to finance solutions to the world's serious problems and other initiatives that support the common good. Business will retain the remaining portion of the funds generated through collaboration. This portion will be divided among the segment firms in proportion to their individual contributions to the fund.

As a result, each business will have the wealth generated by its individual efforts and a portion of the wealth created through collaborative initiatives. In this way, each firm will earn more than it possibly could by operating alone without collaborating, and its share of the additional wealth will come courtesy of the other firms' efforts. This approach will align the entire industry segment with dedicating itself to the achievement of full coordination and cooperation.

Clear Path to Collaboration

By applying the previously discussed structural approach to eliminating the win/loss dynamics and maximizing inter-firm coordination and collaboration, it should be possible to ensure that no firm in an industry segment will lose as a result of another's gain. Further, the dynamics created will provide that all firms will benefit from each other's successes. This path to collaboration should be clear, since no unaddressed serious structural reasons remain for firms to avoid coordination and cooperation. Additionally, the proposed structural rationalization should make it easier for individual firms to achieve mastery of their core business, as discussed in Chapter Two. The examples in Chapter Three illustrate that even without such structural changes, direct competitors will collaborate when mutual benefit can be achieved. In such cases, the individual firms involved can look past their differences and work as a team, if they are not required to give up the key source of individual competitiveness. As shown in the case of Daimler and BMW, combined component sourcing does not affect the areas of significant competitive differentiation between the two lines of vehicles.

However, many firms probably lack the degree of predisposition toward collaboration exhibited by Daimler and BMW. So, for widespread adoption of GEO, a collective cognitive shift is needed to create the whole-hearted willingness to undertake the necessary structural changes and to pursue a win/win rather than win/lose approach to business. This cognitive shift will fully enliven the cooperative spirit, which is the basis of collaborative behavior. Chapter Eleven will discuss this cognitive change and show how its achievement will pave the way for adoption of GEO. But first, Chapter Four will present how the global business sphere will function under the influence of the new Global Economic Optimization paradigm.

Chapter Four
A New Paradigm
for the Global Business Sphere

This book presents a new paradigm for the global business sphere—Global Economic Optimization (GEO). This paradigm rests on the foundation of coordination and cooperation among the firms in each of the world's industry segments fostered by business interactions that eliminate win/loss events and retain only win, win situations. A chief benefit of this new business paradigm is its ability to generate vast additional wealth beyond that currently produced by our present economic model. This benefit is very timely given our present global economic malaise and rapidly approaching socio-ecological difficulties.

Because the benefits of coordination and cooperation are achievable in any group activity, we must define "business" broadly enough to apply this new paradigm as widely as possible. In this way we will achieve the maximum possible wealth-generative effect for the world. To accomplish this goal, we will include all of the applicable arenas in the North American Industry Classification System, including: Agriculture, Forestry, Fishing, Mining/Quarrying/Oil and Gas Extraction, Utilities, Construction, Manufacturing, Wholesale Trade, Retail Trade, Transportation and Warehousing, Information, Finance and Insurance, Real Estate/Rental/Leasing, Professional/Scientific/Technical Services, Management of Companies and Enterprises, Administrative Services, Support Services, Waste Management Services, Remediation Services, Educational Services, Health Care and Social Assistance, Arts/Entertainment/Recreation, Accommodation and Food Services, and Public Administration.[82] The terms "segment" and "firm" will be flexible. For example, we may refer to public secondary-level and private primary-level education as segments and individual schools as firms within those segments. The students attending the schools would be analogous to customers.

In all of the arenas above, the infusion of coordination and cooperation will bring the greatest wealth-generative benefit to segments with the largest number of firms and the greatest overall segment revenues because more firms generate more lines of coordination and cooperation within the segment (see Chapter Three). Also, the achievable forms of collaboration have potentially more impact in a larger segment.

GEO, the new economic approach presented here, has some key considerations. In this model, the infusion of coordination and cooperation into the global business sphere, creates three general categories of coexisting industry segments that vary according to their ability to benefit from collaboration. The use of widespread collaboration in the "business" sphere will generate vast additional wealth and newly available human resources. The added wealth will be used to (1) fund solutions for the world's serious problems, (2) to provide incentives to those whose efforts produce added wealth, and (3) to fund the development of innovative new technologies, products, and services. The human resources will receive job opportunities in projects that address the world's problems or in initiatives that develop and produce new technologies, products, or services. Figure 19 illustrates the basic elements of Global Economic Optimization.

To provide a deeper understanding of GEO, we will now discuss its basic characteristics in greater detail.

Three General Categories of Coexisting Industry Segments

Industry Segments with Little Benefit from Coordination and Cooperation

The world's many industry segments are varyingly suited to infusion of coordination and cooperation. Segments with few suppliers and small or infant markets have little to gain from collaboration. This category includes ventures that are in the initial stages of developing new technologies, products, and services. Such firms are typically one of a kind or are among a small handful of similarly focused enterprises that have not yet commercialized their offering or have just started to do so. Due to the small number of firms and limited market size, this category of industry segment has very few lines of potential inter-firm cooperation and a small volume of segment

Global Economic Optimization

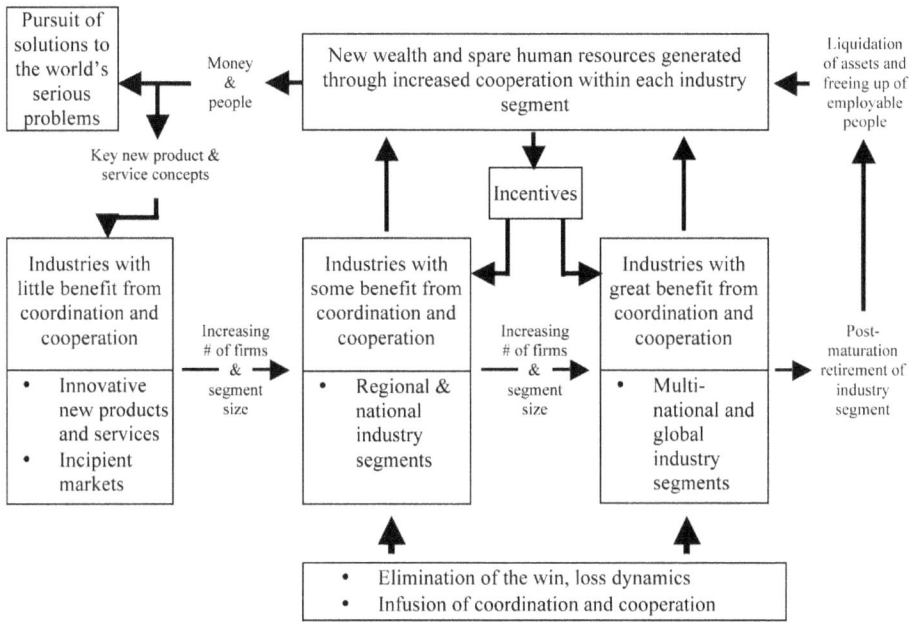

Figure 19.

revenues over which to leverage cooperative initiatives. Consequently, such situations will not yet be able to generate significant additional wealth beyond that which is individually produced.

However, these smaller types of segments perform a very important role within the grand scheme of GEO by providing a powerful way to ensure optimal ongoing innovation and development of new technologies, products, and services. Innovation will also be spurred within the larger industry segments more suited to coordination and cooperation, but will be applied toward enhancement of the products and services already offered in those segments. This is appropriate and necessary so that adequate emphasis is given to those segments promising more effect toward the generation of additional wealth. However, our first category of incipient industry segments offers an opportunity beyond maximizing the creation of additional wealth. This category optimizes the development of new technologies, products, and services so that the world moves into a more positive future at the fastest possible speed. This will provide a great advantage over our present business model in which each firm's attention and financial resources are stretched between meeting quarterly earnings expectations on the one hand and developing life-transforming, paradigm-shifting product concepts on the other.

Industry Segments with Some Benefit from Coordination and Cooperation

The technologies, products, and services developed by the first category of smaller industry segments will either fail or succeed. Successful innovations will create customer demand, new revenues, and a market for the offering. When multiple firms and significant segment-wide revenues develop, the first category industry segment will grow into the second category of larger segments that can gain some benefit from coordination and cooperation. If the new core technology, product, or service fits into an existing segment, it can be incorporated into that segment by first eliminating any serious win/loss dynamics and then instituting the applicable forms of collaboration with the pre-existing firms. If the new core technology, product, or service does not fit into an already existing industry segment, it will become a new second category segment and the appropriate measures can be taken to eliminate the win/loss dynamics and to pursue the appropriate inter-firm collaborative initiatives.

Industry Segments with Great Benefit from Coordination and Cooperation

As the number of firms and revenues grow in a second category segment, it will at some point evolve into a third category segment, capable of benefiting even more from inter-firm coordination and cooperation. Since coordination and collaboration already occurred during the second category segment phase, only monitoring of ongoing functioning will be necessary to identify any arising opportunities to eliminate serious win/loss dynamics or implement additional collaborative initiatives.

Creation of Vast Additional Wealth

As coordination and cooperation in the world's industry segments generate vast additional wealth beyond current practices, the ongoing intent of GEO is to establish a new win/win outcome for <u>all</u> parties concerned. This will produce new and more adequate funding for solving the world's serious problems, help individual firms generate more wealth, and ensure adequate investment in development of the technologies, products, and services capable of carrying civilization comfortably into the future—all of this without creating any negative socio-ecological side effects.

Much of the additional wealth created will be allocated to solving the world's serious problems, as we will need to repair and, in some cases, rebuild the foundation upon which life will progress. Lesser, but adequate, newly-created wealth will be used to fund future-oriented development initiatives. The remaining portion of the additional wealth will go to the individual firms that fully dedicate themselves to this new paradigm based on inter-firm coordination and cooperation.

Funding for Solutions to the World's Serious Problems

The introduction of this book indicated that our world is struggling with economic problems and facing rapidly approaching socio-ecological difficulties. The economic crisis consumed individual, business, and governmental financial reserves. Economic bailout spending amounted to more than a trillion dollars in the United States alone.[83] Prior to the onset of our economic problems, the cost of addressing the world's socio-ecological difficulties was estimated at several hundred billion dollars annually.[84] Even if our economies return to pre-crisis growth levels, significant time will be needed to rebuild the reserves necessary to address our socio-ecological challenges. Unfortunately, spending is needed on all fronts right now to address problems that are still somewhat contained and reversible. GEO can create the additional wealth needed to address our increasing difficulties and to set the world back on the path of progress.

Incentives for those Working to Create the Added Wealth

The shift from our existing win/loss dynamics to the win/win paradigm capable of generating vast additional wealth will require much hard work. The firms and individuals that embrace this undertaking to the benefit of all will need to be properly compensated for their service.

Those who believe that greed and the unbridled self-interest of business have created many of our economic and socio-ecological woes may have a critical view of such compensation. Clearly elements of the prevailing business ethic have contributed to the world's problems, and paying exorbitant bonuses to already wealthy individuals who may have helped damage the common good is unconscionable.

However, the firms and individuals that GEO will reward are those who embrace the paradigm of coordination and cooperation so that all can win, rather than a few greedy individuals who are willing to prosper at the expense of others' misfortune and suffering. Therefore, GEO will track the degree of each firm's efforts toward coordination and cooperation, as well as its actual contribution to the added wealth being generated through collaboration. Dedicated participating firms will be allowed to retain a portion of the generated additional wealth. A possible approach to achieve this end is the creation of an annual budget to cover the costs of funding solutions to the world's problems and to develop future technologies, products and services. Firms would contribute to this budgeted amount only from the additional wealth generated by inter-firm collaboration, not from their stand alone efforts. Each firm would contribute the extra wealth it generated through collaboration until the annual budget for funding the above two pursuits is reached. At that point, the companies would retain a hundred percent of every profit dollar. Through GEO, companies would generate more wealth through inter-firm collaboration than through the present minimally collaborative approach to business. In order to track the wealth generated through collaboration, each firm would be required to report such earnings on its financial statements as project income, with clear notations indicating the identities of the co-collaborators, as well as the nature of the collaboration. Consequently, each contributing firm would become richer through coordination and cooperation (GEO), than through pursuing only its own interests.

Likewise, individuals within the industry segment who made obvious efforts to render outstanding contributions to the creation of additional wealth would receive bonuses to acknowledge their achievements. Even though such acknowledgements of individual and firm contribution would be significant, they would make up only a portion of the total additional wealth created.

Funding for Development of Innovative New Technologies, Products, and Services

Ongoing advances in technology have spurred much of civilization's progress. The ideas of individuals like the Wright brothers, Nikola Tesla, and Albert Einstein, while clearly ahead of their times, have resulted in present-day conditions unimagined during their lifetimes. Present day glimpses into the potentialities of new fields such as nanotechnology[85] and genomics/genetic engineering[86] indicate that technological advancement is likely to continue to drive progress. No doubt, the most effective solutions for many of our problems and the keys to future conveniences lie in adequate funding of the development of new technologies, products and services. Without such funding we will not move forward as quickly or safely as possible, since substantial study and testing are necessary to ensure that emerging new ideas are understood fully enough to prevent any undesirable and unforeseen side effects.

This category of funding will be a powerful complement to the business sphere's current ongoing investment in research and development (R&D). Due to the pressures presently exerted by stakeholders and financial markets, businesses must focus R&D spending on the achievement of shorter term financial objectives. As a result, a bias exists toward addressing the most important issues only to the extent that they are also most urgent. Consequently our current long-term needs and interests are often neglected. Increased R&D funding through GEO will mitigate this situation by ensuring that both the urgent and important areas of technological, product, and service development are adequately funded and addressed.

Newly Available Human Resources

The present win/loss nature of business discourages firms from coordinating and cooperating with one another. This causes a great deal of redundancy in the business sphere as firms each maintain all necessary support functions rather than share common resources with one another. Part of this problem exists in the area of human resources. Infusion of inter-firm coordination and collaboration will free up significant numbers of workers whose present jobs will no longer be necessary. Fortunately, GEO will create many new jobs in the process of eliminating the redundancies inherent in our present approach. These new jobs will support vital new initiatives that have not yet received the required attention. Some examples of such unaddressed pursuits are listed below:

- Development of sources of alternative energy
- Management of the effects of global climate change
- Response to impacts of extreme weather events/natural calamities
- Pollution control
- Elimination of abject poverty
- Population control
- Disease control in an increasingly densely populated world
- New infrastructure to mirror population growth and continued urbanization
- Building of new infrastructure
- Repair/replacement of aging existing infrastructure
- Preservation/replenishment of fresh water supplies
- Increased food production and food safety
- Preservation of ecological diversity
- Technology development for all of the above

GEO will create both newly available human resources and newly generated wealth needed to pursue these previously unaddressed initiatives. The newly generated wealth will fund capital expenditures to equip the projects and to train and compensate the workers. Since much of the staff formerly held jobs eliminated due to redundancy, re-training will be an important issue. While one individual's new job may not require training, another individual may need significant preparation for his/her new assignment. The possible training scenarios are shown in Figure 20.

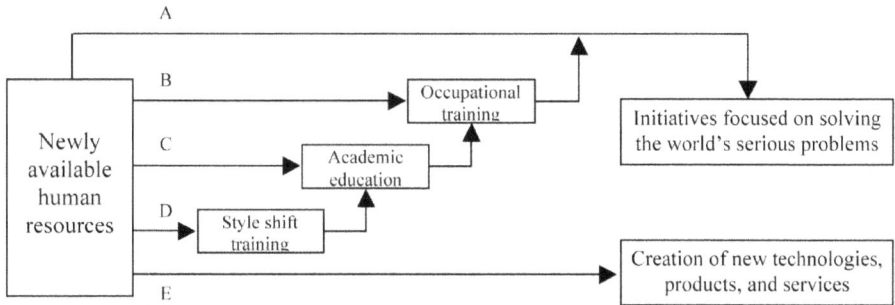

Figure 20.

As is indicated in track A above, some individuals may require no re-training due to strong similarities between their former and new jobs. For example, a mechanical engineer whose gasoline-powered auto design job became redundant may need no retraining to assume a new position designing alternative fuel-powered automobiles. However, as suggested in track B, the same mechanical engineer may need specific occupational training if the new job is focused on alternative fuel-powered off-highway vehicles requiring heavier duty construction. Additional academic education will likely be necessary if, as suggested by track C, the design engineer's new position is in manufacturing process engineering rather than product design engineering. Following the additional academic work, the engineer will likely need job specific occupational training. The change to the new job may require a shift in fundamental behavioral style, as is suggested by track D. For example, the move from mechanical design engineer to sales engineer may require the individual to exhibit a more outgoing and sociable demeanor than previously. While such stylistic changes may be more difficult to master, they are possible through practices that make individuals more aware of their latent personality attributes.[87] Following completion of stylistic shift training, the individual may require additional academic education, and finally job-specific occupational training.

Some holders of redundant jobs may become the conceptualizers of innovative new technologies, products, and services. Eliminating their redundant jobs will free them to pursue development of these ideas. While they may not need any specific re-training, funds will be available for them to

develop new ideas that are deemed worthwhile and actionable by those pos-
sessing skill in evaluating new ventures.

By funding new ventures and applying the appropriate forms of re-
training for new positions, each individual should be able to assume a new
role that is not redundant and that gifts us with some new technology/prod-
uct/service or contribution to the solution of some of the world's serious
problems.

Post-Maturation Retirement of Industry Segments

Once an industry segment has passed maturity and is replaced by more
time-appropriate product and/or service counterparts, its useful life cycle
will end. If adequate funding of the products, services, and technologies of
the future is feeding the "front end" of the GEO model, prolonging the life
of a "spent" industry segment merely to perpetuate its no longer needed
jobs will not be necessary. Instead, the industry's physical assets can be liq-
uidated and the freed-up capital and human resources can be redeployed to
projects focused on solving the world's serious socio-ecological problems
or developing key new products, services, and technological concepts.

The vast additional wealth generated through GEO will be well used,
as follows:

- To provide the funds needed to solve the world's serious socio-
  ecological problems

- To create incentives for those accomplishing the shift from
  the business sphere's win/loss dynamics to a coordinated and
  cooperative win/win approach

- To fund the development of innovative new technologies, products,
  and services

- To pay for the re-training of individuals who move to new and
  more purposeful jobs following elimination of their redundant
  positions

But, these benefits can be achieved only if the proper governance structure
is established. The next chapter will present a governance structure capable
of ensuring that GEO accomplishes the economic miracle for which it is
intended.

Chapter Five
The Appropriate Governance Structure

The establishment of inter-firm coordination and cooperation under GEO will require a significant paradigm shift away from our current win/loss dynamics. A shared common vision within the world's business sphere will be needed to ensure that a change of such great magnitude can be achieved in a synchronized manner.

Despite the temptation to employ a top/down governance structure to communicate and impose the vision throughout the business sphere, such an approach would be doomed to failure. Top/down governance deprives decision making of critical information that resides at the foundational levels of an organization, and destroys the sense of ownership and initiative crucial to ensure that all parties are fully interested and engaged in achievement of the agreed upon common goal.[88] Full buy-in of all involved will enliven the full wealth-generative potential of GEO.

The ideal governance structure must nurture maximum individual initiative while aligning the intentions and efforts of all with a common vision. Figure 21 on the following page illustrates a governance structure that will be capable of reconciling these potentially divergent objectives at the individual industry segment level. In the interest of simplicity, a mere six-firm segment is shown.

Governance Structure at the Level of the Individual Industry Segment

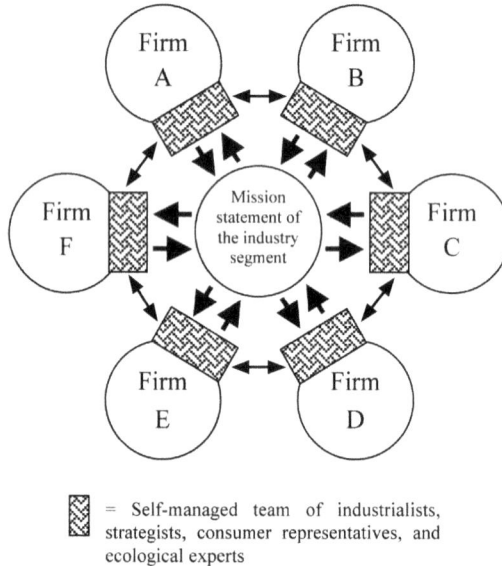

Figure 21.

The preceding figure illustrates a governance structure with the following characteristics:

- A commonly agreed upon mission statement of the industry segment to be used as a point of reference by each firm
- Self-managed teams of industrialists, strategists, consumer representatives, and ecological experts functioning within each of the segment's firms
- Coordination of the self-managed teams

Further discussion of these attributes is useful to deepen our understanding of the segment-level governance structure.

A Commonly Agreed-Upon Mission Statement of the Industry Segment to Be Used as a Point of Reference by Each Firm

Under the influence of GEO each industry segment will have a collectively agreed-upon mission statement. This mission statement will serve as the point of reference that aligns each firm with segment goals and coordinates all firms in the segment. Each mission statement will have unique elements, but all segment missions will have three factors in common:

- Optimization of the wealth-generative capacity of the segment as a whole
- Promotion of reasonable consumer interests relating to product/ service choice and cost
- Adherence to acceptable standards of socio-ecological sustainability

Therefore, all firm strategies and initiatives will be designed to maximize coordination and collaboration without opposing the interests of customers, society, or the environment. Without a segment-wide mission statement that emphasizes such values, a segment's firms may be excessively self-interested, un-coordinated, and less than fully aligned with the common good.

Self-managed Teams of Industrialists, Strategists, Consumer Representatives, and Ecological Experts Functioning within Each of the Segment's Firms

Each firm will have a non-hierarchically structured self-managed team of industrialists, strategists, consumer representatives, and ecological experts to align the firm's strategies and initiatives with the principal elements of the segment mission that includes the optimization of inter-firm collaboration to maximize overall segment wealth.

The prescribed composition of each self-managed team will ensure that maximization of segment wealth occurs in synchrony with promotion of customer, societal and environmental interests. Since teams will include business people, customer representatives, and ecological experts, all critical perspectives will be addressed concurrently rather than sequentially, to ensure the most efficient decision making/planning process.

The use of non-hierarchical self-managed teams will foster a greater sense of ownership and initiative than a more top/down approach and, therefore, create maximum enthusiasm directed toward achievement of the segment mission.

Coordination of the Self-Managed Teams from All Firms

In addition to aligning firm strategies and initiatives with the segment mission, all self-managed teams will promote a high degree of coordination and collaboration with each other. Consequently, all teams will continually pursue all opportunities for eliminating win/loss dynamics and maximizing collaboration with one another.

The absence of any significant level of governance higher than the individual industry segment will support the functioning of self-management. However, support will be available to the industry segments in the form of mentoring, as well as the auditing and reporting of segment results to encourage achievement of segment objectives. These capabilities are shown in Figure 22 on the facing page.

By thoroughly discussing the schematic shown above we can more fully appreciate the role of the macro-level resources that will support GEO.

Mentoring to Encourage
Achievement of Segment Objectives

The industry segment will have coordination among the self-managed teams of each firm. As a result, firms will be able to work together toward elimination of the win/loss dynamics within the segment and maximization of inter-firm collaboration. Yet, each firm will be somewhat bound by its individual perspective and may, as a result, struggle at times to see the "big picture" of segment-wide cooperation. To compensate for this, Global Economic Optimization Mentoring Resource will assist each segment. This mentoring resource will stand as an objective third party with an overall view, more poised to see the full possibilities of collaboration from a broader perspective than is possible for the segment's firms. This mentoring resource will work with each segment to ensure that the clearest and most comprehensive

Macro-Level Support for Achievement of Segment Objectives

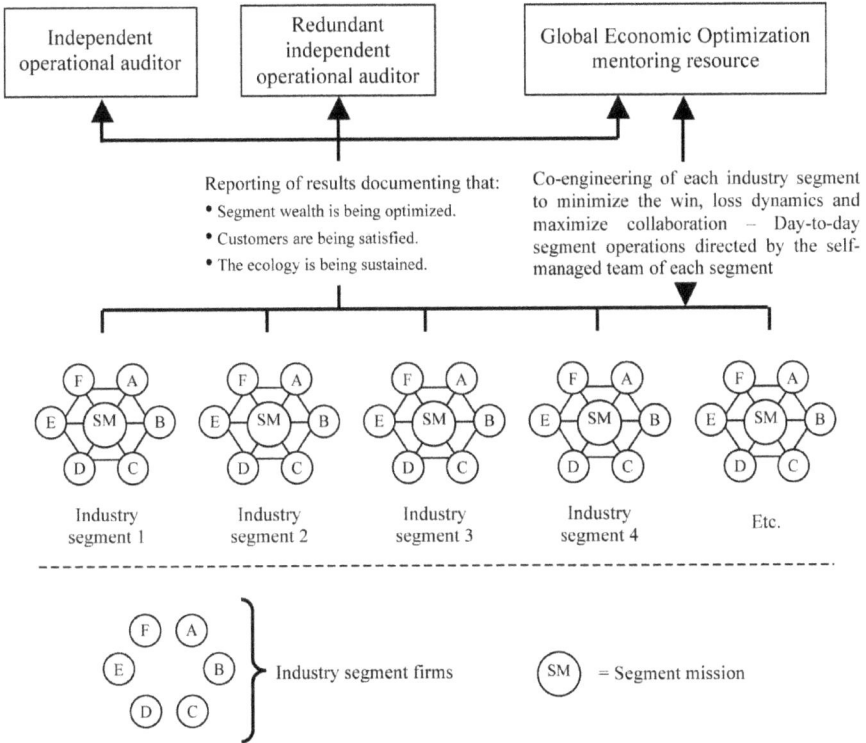

Figure 22.

vision of segment collaboration is available to the segment's firms as they strive to realize the segment's full wealth-generative potential.

The firms of the segment will not have formal reporting responsibility to the mentoring resource. As a result, the self-management of the segment and its firms will prevail along with the corresponding inspiration and motivation of the parties involved.

Auditing and Reporting of Segment Operational Results

Each industry segment will report its results separately to each of two independent auditing organizations. Reported results will reveal the degree to which each segment achieves wealth generation, customer satisfaction, and ecological sustainability. Reporting these results to each organization separately will maximize the transparency of the results of each segment and serve to ensure accuracy and integrity.

Segment results will be released on a continuous basis to all stakeholders including the business people and customers of all segments and the public at large. Everyone in these groups will have a vested interest in the effective implementation of GEO and will benefit from the resulting maximization of global wealth that simultaneously upholds socio-ecological values. It is this added wealth that will provide funding of solutions to the world's serious problems. The stakeholders will be encouraged to make their voices heard if they believe that accomplishments are not optimal. This will foster a significant additional incentive for industry segments to work conscientiously toward the maximization of segment wealth and the satisfaction of customer and socio-ecological interests.

The Role of Government

While government may have some degree of responsibility for the general well being of its citizens, GEO is not intended to be a government run program. Unlike socialistic and communistic models, the new approach being presented in this book does not involve state ownership of the means of production or any form of state planning. All planning, decision making and governance is generated from within the business sphere itself. Of course, the judicial branch of government will enforce statutes related to contractual relationships and the management and appropriation of funds; but that will be the only role for government. This is good news for those who generally oppose initiatives that call for a stronger government role.

Government will be asked to support the pursuit of coordination and cooperation in the business sphere, since such efforts will create vast additional wealth and fund solutions to the world's serious problems. This added wealth and its successful appropriation will go far to satisfy government's heartfelt desire to ensure the wellbeing of its people. Therefore, government should gladly do its part to promote and support the GEO initiative without actually controlling it.

In our present approach, competition is used to uphold customer interests. But GEO will infuse a high degree of coordination and collaboration into the business sphere. Customer interests will be effectively pursued through other, less costly means. Even so, some redefinition of the existing regulations and refocusing of the agencies that deal with competition in the business sphere will be needed. Currently, such entities monitor the field of business to ensure that inter-firm collaboration does not result in excessive prices or reduced customer options regarding products and services. Although GEO maximizes collaboration, the interests of customers <u>and</u> those of society and the environment will be enhanced beyond what they are with our existing approach to business. Monitoring will need to be shifted from minimization to maximization of collaboration. GEO provides for an independent non-governmental monitoring entity to ensure that this happens. It may well be that the individuals most immediately qualified to staff this organization will be those who currently work for the government on the side of limiting inter-firm cooperation. They already understand the mechanics of collaboration and would need only a re-definition of their mission.

Chapter Six
Collecting, Distributing, and Monitoring the Additional Wealth

GEO will annually generate many trillions of dollars of additional wealth. That wealth will be used to fund solutions for the world's serious problems, to provide incentives to those whose efforts contribute to the added wealth, and to fund the development of innovative new technologies, products, and services. Our survival and continued progress in life depends on the success of this undertaking. Therefore, effective collection, distribution, and monitoring of the additional wealth must be ensured to accomplish these vital goals. The high degree of transparency and accountability required is depicted in Figure 23 which illustrates several features needed to guarantee that the newly created wealth achieves its intended purpose.

Discussion of the schematic will highlight the conditions necessary to ensure that the added wealth generated through GEO achieves its intended purpose.

Collection of the Additional Wealth in a Dedicated Special Fund

Through GEO each industry segment will generate substantial sums of additional wealth via inter-firm coordination and collaboration. The wealth generated over and above that created without collaboration will flow into a dedicated special fund to prevent commingling. This will simplify tracking the additional wealth and monitoring the extent to which coordination and collaboration are achieving their objective. This special fund will be the "bank" to fund legitimate pursuits.

Collection, Distribution, and Monitoring of the Additional Wealth

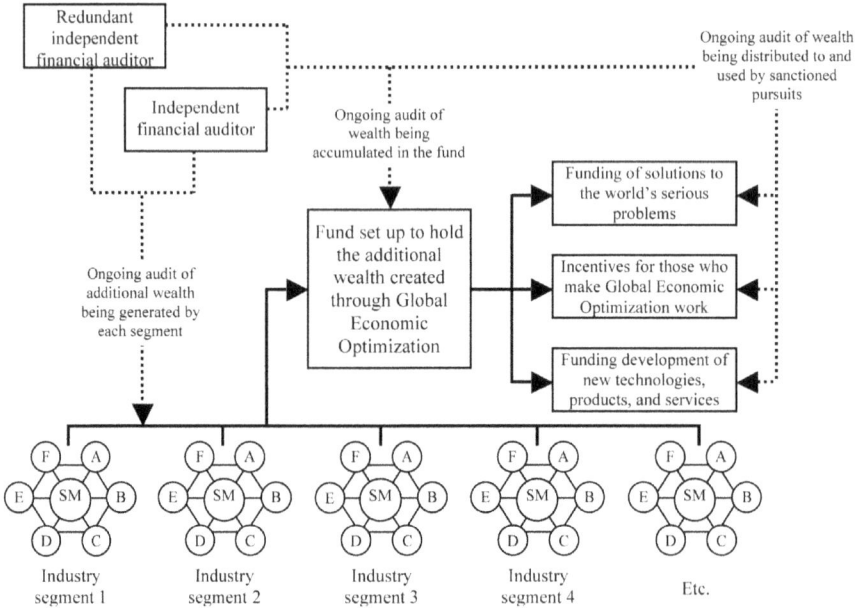

Figure 23.

Distribution of the Additional
Wealth to Worthwhile Pursuits

The dedicated special fund will finance solutions for the world's serious problems, provide incentives to those whose efforts result in the added wealth, and fund the development of innovative new technologies, products, and services. A review committee composed of individuals qualified to determine the fundability of the requests brought before them will represent each of these three areas. The committee responsible for funding solutions to the world's serious problems will include individuals capable of determining the viability, cost effectiveness, and speed of implementation of each proposed solution. The committee responsible for providing incentives to the firms and individuals responsible for GEO's success will include individuals who fully understand the forms of collaboration and can objectively measure firm and individual contributions to the added wealth, customer satisfaction, and socio-ecological sustainability. The committee responsible for funding pursuit of innovative new technologies, products, and services will be comprised of skilled venture capitalists with know-how that qualifies them to determine the viability and future impact of new ideas.

An individual or entity will only receive funds once the guidelines of the appropriate committee have been met, but the processing of requests will be made in a non-bureaucratic, results oriented and timely manner.

Monitoring of the Additional Wealth from Inception through Utilization

Given the magnitude of the funds that will be generated through GEO, the highest levels of transparency and accountability must prevail throughout the process of administering the wealth. This will be the focus of two fully independent financial auditing organizations, unrelated to any participants in GEO to minimize influence from any vested interests. They will also be independent of one another and perform identical audits of the same information, without comparing notes prior to the simultaneous release of their separate audit results. Any discrepancies in the two audits will signal a need for deeper investigation by the legal system.

Both entities will perform the same four audits: (1) audit of the additional wealth being generated by each industry segment, (2) audit of the added wealth being accumulated in the dedicated special fund, (3) audit of the decisions of the committees that approve the release of funds to legitimate pursuits, and (4) audit of the use of the funds by the individuals or entities that have received portions of the fund's wealth.

Audit of the Additional Wealth Being Generated by Each Industry Segment Each audit entity will separately review the amount of additional wealth being generated by each industry segment. This is the amount resulting directly from the various forms of collaboration pursued within the segment. These audits will verify that the appropriate amount of wealth was contributed to the dedicated special fund.

Audit of the Added Wealth Being Accumulated in the Dedicated Special Fund Each audit entity will also check the amount of accumulated wealth in the dedicated special fund to ensure that the fund decreases are equal to the distributions to approved legitimate pursuits.

Audit of the Decisions of Committees that Approve the Release of Funds to Legitimate Pursuits   Lastly, each audit entity will review the decisions of the committees that approve funding to ensure that (1) the endeavors are legitimate (2) the proposed solutions to world problems are viable, cost effective, and achievable in a reasonable timeframe (3) that the individuals and organizations recognized for their contributions to GEO made significant contributions and (4) the proposed new technologies, products, and services are important, realistic, cost effective, and socio-ecologically friendly.

Audit of the Use of the Funds by the Individuals or Entities that have Received Funding   Finally, each audit entity will review the progress being made on the funded solutions to world problems and on the development of the funded new technologies, products, and services. The goal is to determine if the pursuits are still viable and if expected cost and completion-time objectives are still deemed achievable. The recommendation may suggest either continuing or terminating funding.

The two audit entities will routinely conduct all four types of audits and remain independent of one another to avoid the possibility of collaboration on the findings. Both entities' audits will be released simultaneously to the public at large to ensure that all sectors of society know the progress of industrial collaboration at the same time.

The indicated program of audits will maximize transparency regarding the collection, distribution, and monitoring of the additional wealth generated through GEO, and strengthen the likelihood that the accumulating funds are used for the intended purposes.

Chapter Seven
Opportunities for Ownership and Investment

The current business paradigm views individual firms as the primary wealth generative entities with little or no significance attributed to the industry segment at large. As a result, we commonly consider only individual firms as objects of both ownership and investment, not the industry segments within which firms operate.

Under the influence of GEO, individual firms and their shareholders will still own the equity value represented by their assets, but inter-firm coordination and cooperation characteristic of GEO raises the possibility that enormous additional wealth could be attributed to the industry segment at large. This could allow the segment itself to be viewed as a vehicle of both ownership and investment. As a result, issues should be discussed regarding ownership and investment considerations that have not been relevant previously.

Ownership Issues

When operated as an environment that promotes inter-firm coordination and collaboration, the industry segment will generate substantial additional wealth and could possess equity value beyond that of the segment's firms. While the bulk of the segment's accumulated additional wealth will be used to benefit the world at large, some of the added wealth should remain in the Special Dedicated Fund mentioned in Chapter Six, to address particular issues related to ownership.

As Chapter Three described, adjustments will be required to eliminate the most serious instances of the win/ loss dynamics from the global business sphere, so that the world's firms will be willing to wholeheartedly pursue their opportunities for coordination and cooperation. Some of these adjustments may result in modifications to some firm's product portfolios, customer lists, or physical assets. These modifications could reduce a firm's value to the extent that it lessens product portfolio, customer list or physical assets.

If a firm has agreed to the reductions in order to maximize the industry segment's wealth generative potential, the shareholders of the firm should not suffer a reduction of their equity value. To avoid such a reduction, the shareholders of the value-diminished firm would be awarded a reconciling amount of non-voting equity in the industry segment at large.

Investment Issues

Currently individuals and institutions invest in individual firms and groups of firms, such as sector funds and mutual funds. The return from the investment is related to performance of the individual firm or group of firms. The present win/loss dynamics of the business sphere increases the uncertainty of firm performance because firms must fend for themselves, unaided by the other firms within the relevant industry segment. Not only do firms face the costs and challenges of business alone, but direct competitors often work overtly and covertly to derail each other's efforts. Even when firms do not make a conscious effort to thwart each other, the lack of communication and coordination of strategies increases the likelihood that the actions of one will interfere with the efforts of another. To a significant extent the winner achieves its status at the expense of its competing firms. All of these factors increase the risk that a firm will not perform as desired.

In a better scenario, coordinated and collaborative GEO firms will share the costs, know-how, and best practices related to all conceivable areas of business. They will not intentionally or inadvertently thwart each other's initiatives. The coordination of strategies, know-how, and resources will equip segment firms with the strength and resourcefulness to deal more effectively with unforeseen circumstances, such as adverse weather conditions or natural disasters.

This will mitigate much of the risk of business and result in steadier performance of individual firms and the industry segments they occupy. This, in turn, should yield more consistently desirable results for individual and institutional investors who are betting on positive firm performance. Improved investment appreciation driven by increased strength and consistency should decrease the need for investment practices that hedge against firm or sector failure.

Beyond the current opportunity to invest in individual firms and certain groups of firms, GEO will afford the ability to invest in newly created indices as follows:

- any of the vast number of industry segments present in the global business sphere, on a national, regional, or global basis
- the aggregate of all industry segments present in the global business sphere, on a national, regional, or global basis

More than Just Enhanced Opportunities for Investment

Infusing coordination and collaboration into the global business sphere will produce a broader range of investment opportunities and a steadier, less risky investment climate. To further maximize the benefits of reduced risk, it may be necessary to legislate limits on the degree to which greed-motivated investment practices can negatively impact financial markets and destroy the wealth of individuals and institutions. This book does not immediately address such reform, but such safeguards would enable GEO to establish an even more powerful means for wealth accumulation through investment. However, the benefits of GEO go far beyond the enhancement of investment opportunities by offering the world the far reaching, profound benefits discussed at length in the next chapter.

Chapter Eight
A More Unified World

GEO will generate vast additional wealth to benefit mankind and avert great difficulties on the path of progress, but other powerful consequences will also result.

Beyond Connectedness to Coordination and Cooperation

In this world, we cannot help but impact each other by our actions. This was so even in 1900 when the world population was only 1.6 billion[89] and our modes of transportation and communication were far less developed than at present. It is far truer today with 6.77 billion[90] people on Earth and with transportation, telecommunications and computing technologies so advanced that events occurring on one side of the planet affect the other side in a matter of seconds. The global economic crisis precipitated in 2008 painfully illustrates this hyper-connectedness. Unsound business practices[91] in the U.S. quickly transmitted a destabilizing effect throughout the world's financial markets.

The extra time and space we enjoyed a century ago has given way to immediacy and close proximity. The world has become a profoundly connected and dynamically interactive system. This state of heightened connectedness is extremely dangerous because it greatly exceeds our degree of coordination. Without coordination, our interactions are more random, less purposeful and less cooperative and will inevitability lead to undesirable chain reactions. Unless we take steps to create heightened coordination in the world, we will not be able to avoid precipitating disaster on each other or to respond effectively to economic difficulties and socio-ecological challenges such as earthquakes, extreme weather, and pandemic illnesses.

Based on its win/loss dynamics, the business sphere is one of the forces opposing the achievement of a more coordinated world. Firms have worked intentionally against other firms and our socio-ecological best interests. Nations have pursued their own interests without enough consideration to the impact on other nations. GEO promises to create an extraordinary degree of coordination and cooperation within the business sphere that will infuse commerce and the economy with sufficient coordination to accommodate the heightened level of connectedness in the world. Additionally, GEO will help to de-emphasize the factors that divide us and encourage coordination and cooperation in various arenas of life beyond business and economy.

Minimization of the Issues that Divide Us

With minor exceptions, differing philosophies, religious beliefs, economic requirements, cultural values, political orientations, and national/regional loyalties have long divided our world. Conflicts ranging from localized disagreements, to brutal global wars, have arisen when the factors that divided us became greater than those we held in common. We need to create a dynamic that allows us to effectively pursue our shared objectives while supporting our diversity.

The infusion of coordination and cooperation will naturally enhance our understanding of how to work together and minimize the factors that divide us. Let us consider how GEO may help us grow in unity despite our differences.

Differing Philosophies, Religious Beliefs, Economic Requirements, Cultural Values, Political Orientations, and National or Regional Loyalties

Each person possesses a unique set of philosophies and beliefs, cultural identities, political persuasions, and national or regional loyalties, and economic requirements. These factors tend to both unite and divide us. The orientations of any two individuals may either affirm or antagonize their relationship. If the individuals' orientations conflict, obstacles to working together may arise that can result in antagonism, conflict and failed initiatives.

The Mitigation of Our Differences

The win/loss dynamics of the global business sphere is a strong factor that divides us and weakens our ability to work together toward our shared objectives. GEO promises to eliminate the divisive influence of this win/loss dynamics and infuse the global business sphere with coordination and cooperation. Consequently, formerly competing firms and individuals who previously pursued strategies for winning at the competitor's expense will begin to practice ways to work together to create win/win outcomes for all involved. So, the business sphere that now divides us will, through GEO, become a unifying dynamic that can reduce the divisive influence of our differing philosophies, religious beliefs, cultural values, political orientations, national or regional loyalties, and economic requirements. Consider the following two scenarios. In the first, a Chinese firm and U.S. business are in competition with one another. While firms so geographically divided might not seem to compete, the ongoing process of globalization extends businesses' geographical selling territories to make this increasingly possible. In the second scenario, the same Chinese and US business are in coordination and collaboration with each other.

Scenario 1: Individuals in two *competing* firms, one in China and the other in the U.S. In this scenario, both firms have:
- Vastly different philosophies and religious beliefs
- Very divergent economic expectations
- Different languages and little in common culturally
- Totally different experiences and expectations of government
- Primary loyalty to their own nationalities and identities

They compete against one another at least 50 hours a week and actively pursue the ways of winning at each other's expense

Scenario 2: Individuals in two *collaborating* firms, one in China and one in the U.S. In this scenario, both firms have:
- Vastly different philosophies and religious beliefs
- Very divergent economic expectations
- Different languages and have little in common culturally
- Totally different experiences and expectations of government
- Primary loyalty to their own nationalities and identities

They pursue all means of coordination and collaboration at least 50 hours a week and actively pursue the ways of creating win/win economic outcomes for all parties involved

Obviously, nothing in Scenario 1 will nurture a unifying influence between the two individuals. Their unmitigated dissimilarities will deter them from working together toward common objectives. However, scenario 2 contemplates the adoption of GEO and its characteristic coordination and collaboration. This addition introduces a factor that will build common ground between the two individuals as they work together toward shared economic objectives.

The Critical Need of Our Time

Our once localized economic and socio-ecological difficulties are rapidly becoming global-scale problems we all face. Although the world is now more densely connected, we are not very coordinated or accustomed to working together toward common objectives. As is stated by Professor Jeffrey Sachs in *Common Wealth*, "At the core of our problems today is the collapse of faith in global problem solving and a widespread cynical disbelief in global cooperation itself."[92]

We must remove the gap between connectedness and coordination in order to address the world's serious challenges, many of which began as local problems and grew to planetary proportions that now require our coordinated, global response. GEO's emphasis on coordination and cooperation in the global business sphere will not only generate the additional wealth needed to solve the world's serious problems, but also demonstrate the sorely needed spirit of cooperation that Professor Sachs sees as missing in the world today.

While GEO <u>will</u> demonstrate the spirit of cooperation, Chapter Eleven will reveal that the actual inclination to cooperate will be the result of a collective shift toward a more unified view of life. After all, who will work to implement the full degree of cooperation and coordination contemplated by GEO without first being wholeheartedly motivated? But once the shift to a more unified view does occur, GEO will provide the blueprint for expressing and practicing cooperation and coordination within the global business sphere. This will effectively generate the additional wealth, balance, and harmony needed to ensure our survival and continued progress in life.

Chapter Nine
Misuse of the
Global Business Sphere

To generate the funds needed to effectively address our serious economic and socio-ecological challenges, we must do everything possible to maximize the generation of additional wealth. GEO promises to generate vast additional wealth by infusing coordination and cooperation into the business sphere. Anything short of full pursuit of this goal will be a continued misuse of the global business sphere. As this resource now operates, its focus on pursuit of the common good is seriously lacking.

Coordination and Cooperation
Are Not Comprehensively Optimized

Our global business sphere is characterized by win/loss dynamics rather than coordination or collaboration toward the achievement of shared objectives. Direct competitors work actively against each other's objectives. The business sphere's potential for generating additional wealth, therefore, goes largely untapped.

However, some firms do coordinate their efforts and collaborate in ways that create value beyond what would be possible otherwise. When two firms enter into a strategic alliance, joint venture, merger, or acquisition, they are likely attempting to create added wealth, but the majority of such initiatives fail to achieve this end.[93] Even if all current attempts were successful, misuse of the global business sphere would largely still exist because at present, nothing assures that the two combining firms can generate the most added wealth of any of the possible combinations of firms.

In addition, the combinations that currently occur within an industry segment comprise a small volume of the collaborations that could be pursued. Chapter Three presented evidence that a 35 firm industry segment has 2800 possible opportunities for cooperation by employing just the five most common categories of collaboration. Very few of these 2800 opportunities are actually pursued through M&A initiatives, even in an aggressively consolidating industry segment.

Combinations are pursued to unleash the additional wealth available through coordination and cooperation. The successful combinations accomplish that end. The added wealth then trickles down to the firms' stakeholders and stimulates economic growth in alignment with the stakeholders' preferences.

Unless these successful efforts give significant portions of their added wealth to viable initiatives to address the world's serious problems, most of the benefit goes to a few at the expense of the masses. Ultimately, even the few that benefit will come up short handed when neglected world problems reach catastrophic proportions that challenge even the wealthy. Since the current global business sphere does not directly apply much wealth to solving the world's serious problems, the common good suffers. The few instances of successful coordination and collaboration that occur in today's business sphere are not enough to make a difference.

Individual firms in an industry segment today are by analogy like trees in a forest, and as such "cannot see the forest for the trees". Firms cannot envision how to optimize the full wealth generative potential of the industry segment because they are immersed in the win/loss dynamics that automatically biases them against balancing the common good with their individual self-interest.

Coordination and Cooperation Not Pursued on Behalf of the Common Good

Chapter One presented examples of how the WGTSP principle expresses maximum balance and harmony. Applied to the business sphere, this means, as indicated in figure 24, that firms A, B, and C would naturally maintain the inter-firm communication and coordination (D) necessary to maintain harmony with each other and still pursue their own individual initiatives. This balance would focus its efforts on achieving the common good, that is, the maximization of wealth needed to solve the world's serious problems and ensure progress in life.

As also illustrated, the business sphere presently lacks influence from the WGTSP principle and, therefore, lacks harmony, balance and the ability to achieve its wealth-generative potential. Firms A, B, and C primarily pursue their individual objectives without significant consideration to the inter-firm communication and coordination required to support pursuit of the common good. Individual firm interests are held in such high priority that the common good becomes a mere afterthought. The lack of communication and coordination among competing firms suppresses empathy, promotes fear, and justifies "dog-eat-dog" behavior and the greedy pursuit of individual firm interests over the common good.

Business Sphere Based on the WGTSP Principle

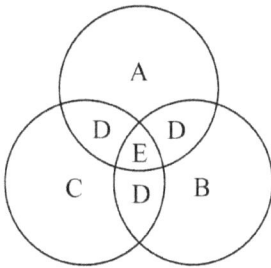

Present Business Sphere Lacking Harmony and Balance

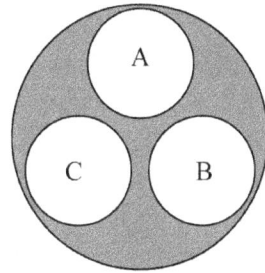

Individual firm interests are balanced with pursuit of the common good through harmonious communication and coordination among firms.

Individual firm interests are out of balance with pursuit of the common good. Lack of communication and coordination promote fear and greed.

Figure 24.

Life is now so interconnected, that any problem can threaten the security of us all, and a lack of progress in any one sphere can retard progress in another. The degree to which we are "all in the same boat" may be less apparent when the problems or pursuits are small and localized, but it becomes decidedly obvious when global problems or pursuits impact our collective security. However, to believe that even small and localized problems do not affect everyone, is to deny the degree of life's interconnectedness.

Acting on the belief that small issues have less impact, allows "minor" issues to grow to global proportions. For example:

- Isolated acts of environmental exploitation seem to have localized
  impact, but these individual acts have compounded to form a
  world-scale problem.
- The birth of one baby at a time has resulted in our world's
  overpopulation.
- Unchecked individual consumption is creating collective energy,
  food, and water shortages.
- Localized tensions and antagonism threaten to escalate into
  global-scale conflict.

A Different Approach is Needed

Given the present nature of things, the expectation that the global business
sphere will be used properly is unrealistic. The win/loss dynamics of business overshadows the importance of tending to the common good by sup-
pressing empathy and fueling fear and greed. But under GEO, firms will
eliminate the win/loss dynamics within each industry segment and collaborate fully among themselves. Freed from being exclusively self-interested,
firms will be able to see their industry segments from a more expansive van-
tage point and work together to develop the vision of how to fully optimize
the wealth generative capacity of the global business sphere. The business
sphere must undergo a shift of perspective in order to free itself of fear and
self-interest enough to see the merit in the pursuit of GEO. This shift will be
discussed fully in Chapter Eleven.

Chapter Ten
Anatomy of an Economic Miracle

Through coordination and cooperation within the world's industry segments, less business assets than are currently employed will create vastly more wealth than is currently generated by our present uncoordinated and non-cooperative approach. Further, this "more from less" effect will simultaneously maximize balance and harmony in the business sphere, economy, and society. The awe and wonder of the potential of this new approach is the reason this book's title refers to GEO as an economic miracle.

The phenomenon that GEO promises repeats a theme that occurs in many areas of life—the whole is greater than the mere sum of its individual parts.[94] In GEO, the wealth generated by individual firms engaged in constructive interaction is greater than the wealth created by the self-interested firms standing alone.

Thus far, this book has presented the various components of this economic miracle. This chapter is dedicated to providing a snapshot of the entire concept and its benefits. It can all come together with one glance at figure 25 on following page.

Figure 25 illustrates the key elements and benefits of GEO. While the previous chapters have discussed these points in depth, the following summary discussion will serve as a companion to the schematic.

The Current Uncoordinated and
Non-cooperative Global business Sphere

Presently inter-firm coordination and cooperation in the global business sphere is minimal. This is surprising given the widespread belief that in many other areas of life, teamwork is the foundation of success. Despite our belief in the virtues of teamwork, businesses operate independently and work actively to thwart each other's initiatives. They compete against each

Global Economic Optimization
Economic Miracle Produced through Coordination and
Cooperation in the Global Business Sphere

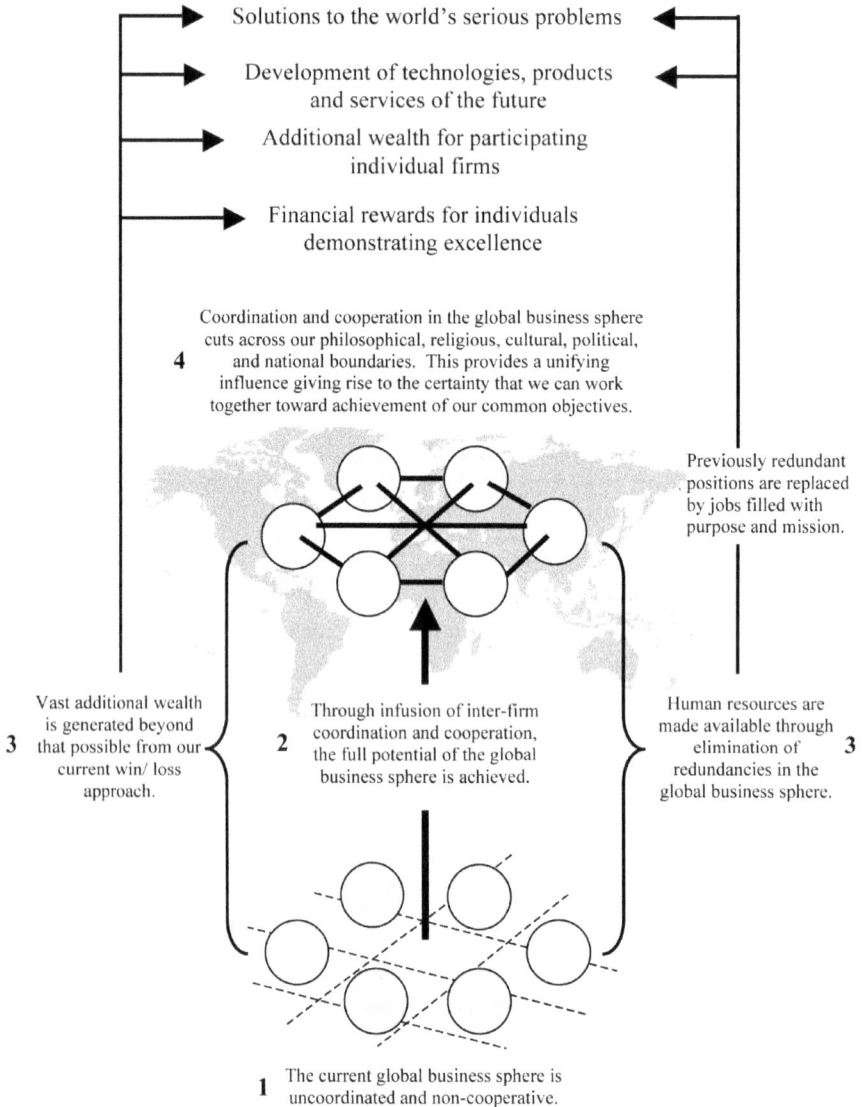

Solutions to the world's serious problems

Development of technologies, products
and services of the future

Additional wealth for participating
individual firms

Financial rewards for individuals
demonstrating excellence

4 Coordination and cooperation in the global business sphere
cuts across our philosophical, religious, cultural, political,
and national boundaries. This provides a unifying
influence giving rise to the certainty that we can work
together toward achievement of our common objectives.

Previously redundant
positions are replaced
by jobs filled with
purpose and mission.

Vast additional wealth
is generated beyond
3 that possible from our
current win/ loss
approach.

2 Through infusion of inter-firm
coordination and cooperation,
the full potential of the global
business sphere is achieved.

Human resources are
made available through
elimination of **3**
redundancies in the
global business sphere.

1 The current global business sphere is
uncoordinated and non-cooperative.

Figure 25.

other for the same customer orders in slow growing markets, especially so given today's tighter economic conditions. This win/loss approach has one firm attempting to succeed at the expense of others. The lack of a more coordinative and collaborative business approach deprives the world of the vast additional wealth that inter-firm cooperation within each industry segment could generate.

Infusion of Coordination and Cooperation to Unfold the Full Potential of the Global Business Sphere

Through inter-firm coordination and cooperation within each of the world's industry segments, the full wealth-generative capacity of the global business sphere can be realized. Coordination and cooperation cannot be wholeheartedly pursued in the present win/loss dynamics of business, so each industry segment must first align itself with a new win/win paradigm in which no firm succeeds at the expense of others. Applying one or more of the adjustments discussed in Chapter Three can accomplish this. Once the appropriate adjustments have been made to each segment, the firms can pursue the opportunities for inter-firm coordination and collaboration. Such opportunities for cooperation will be enormous. As indicated in Chapter Three, as many as 2800 opportunities for collaboration are possible within just one 35 firm industry segment.

Generation of Vast Additional Wealth Beyond that Possible from Our Current Win, Loss Approach

Our current win/loss approach to business pits firm against firm and discourages the teamwork required to realize the full wealth-generative potential of the global business sphere. The coordination and cooperation envisioned in GEO will create many trillions of dollars of additional wealth annually.

Newly Created Additional Wealth Used to Fund Solutions to the World's Serious Problems and to Develop the Technologies, Products, and Services of the Future

The newly created additional wealth will greatly exceed the wealth realized when firms work independently of one another and attempt to thwart each other's success. The added wealth of GEO will allow us to fund solutions to the world's serious problems and to pursue focused development of the technologies, products and services of the future.

Individual Firms Wealthier than Before

A portion of the added wealth will also be allocated to reward the collaborative successes of individual firms and make them even richer as a result of their wholehearted pursuit of collaboration and rejection of the present win/loss approach.

Financial Rewards for Individuals Whose Achievements Contribute Substantially to Accomplishment of Global Economic Optimization

The remaining additional wealth will provide reasonable cash bonuses to those individuals who contribute conspicuously to the achievement of inter-firm coordination and cooperation.

Human Resources Made Available Through Elimination of Redundancies in the Global Business Sphere

Our present win/loss approach to business requires each firm to maintain its own resources and support functions in order to remain competitive. As a result, firms are discouraged from sharing capabilities. This creates an enormously inefficient use of capital and significant redundancies in the area of human resources which contribute significantly to the stifling of the wealth-generative potential of the global business sphere. This situation is especially undesirable given the acute need for additional funding of solutions to our economic and socio-ecological problems and development of the technologies, products, and services of the future. This demands that we pursue all means of generating the money needed to ensure our survival and set the world solidly on the path of optimum progress. This includes the elimination of job redundancies that are depriving the world of a large portion of the money needed to address its serious challenges.

In addition to money, we will need many people to address our economic and socio-ecological challenges. Eliminating job redundancies will provide extra human resources needed to staff the projects focused on solving the world's serious problems and developing the technologies, products, and services of the future. This transition will replace the old redundant jobs with new positions full of purpose and mission.

Unifying Influence that Cuts across Our Philosophical, Religious, Cultural, Political, and National Differences

The philosophical, religious, cultural, political, and national differences that divide us have thwarted our ability to work together in pursuit of our common objectives. As the world becomes more densely populated and highly interactive, working together may offer our only chance of avoiding ultimate catastrophic circumstances such as global economic melt down, conflict, or pandemic illness. Without a strong unifying element we may be unable to overcome our differences enough to develop the necessary collaborative skills. The shift to the highly coordinated and cooperative approach to business as prescribed by GEO will provide a strong unifying influence that can cut across our philosophical, religious, cultural, political, and national differences, and greatly hasten our mastering the ability to cooperate as one people toward achievement of our common objectives.

Miraculous Benefits

Our current economic approach stifles output and fosters imbalance and disharmony both <u>within</u> the business sphere and <u>between</u> business and the interests of society and the environment. GEO will infuse the business sphere with a win/win dynamic in which the efforts of each firm support and magnify those of the others. This approach will produce other win/win benefits as well. Individual firms will become richer while collectively generating the additional wealth needed to solve the world's serious problems—society and the environment both win. Furthermore, many individuals in the workforce will have the opportunity to move beyond redundant positions that presently stifle the world's wealth-generative capacity into new positions full of purpose and mission. Finally, a heightened global-scale focus on development of the technologies, products, and services of the future will ensure that the world will be firmly planted on the path of optimum forward progress. The current global economic malaise denies us of these benefits. GEO will provide the necessary funding without deficit spending, tax increases, or offense to liberal and conservative thinkers who respectively emphasize the need to address our serious problems and to act with fiscal responsibility.

Chapter Eleven
Achievable Reality or Utopian Pipe Dream

Based on the preceding thorough discussion of GEO and its extraordinary potential benefits to mankind, we are ready to consider whether this approach is an achievable reality or some farfetched, utopian pipe dream. Chapter One presented Global Economic Optimization as an application of the WGTSP principle to the global business sphere. The pervasiveness of the WGTSP principle in our lives suggests that its absence from the field of business is an error of omission, not an indication of non-applicability. Additionally, the kinds of successful inter-firm collaborations suggested by GEO have been pursued successfully in the business sphere since the early 1900's. No reason remains to believe that GEO and its benefits are innately unachievable.

Undoubtedly many <u>will</u> embrace GEO as an achievable solution to our serious problems, yet others will reject it as an unachievable fantasy. How can individuals have such contrary views of the same phenomenon? Since the phenomenon is the constant, the source of the variability must be something within the individuals themselves, something that varies from person to person. This key element is the individual cognitive "glasses" with which every person views the external world. Viewed through different glasses, each individual sees the <u>same</u> phenomenon <u>differently</u>.

Cognitive Frameworks

A person's cognitive framework is the basis of his/her world view. The following schematic further illustrates this phenomenon. The diagram presents three cognitive frameworks: Unifying Vision, Transitional Vision, and Polarizing Vision. In each case, "A" represents a point of view embraced by one cognitive type and "B" represents the opposite point of view (for example, big government vs. minimal government, pro-choice vs. pro-life, etc).

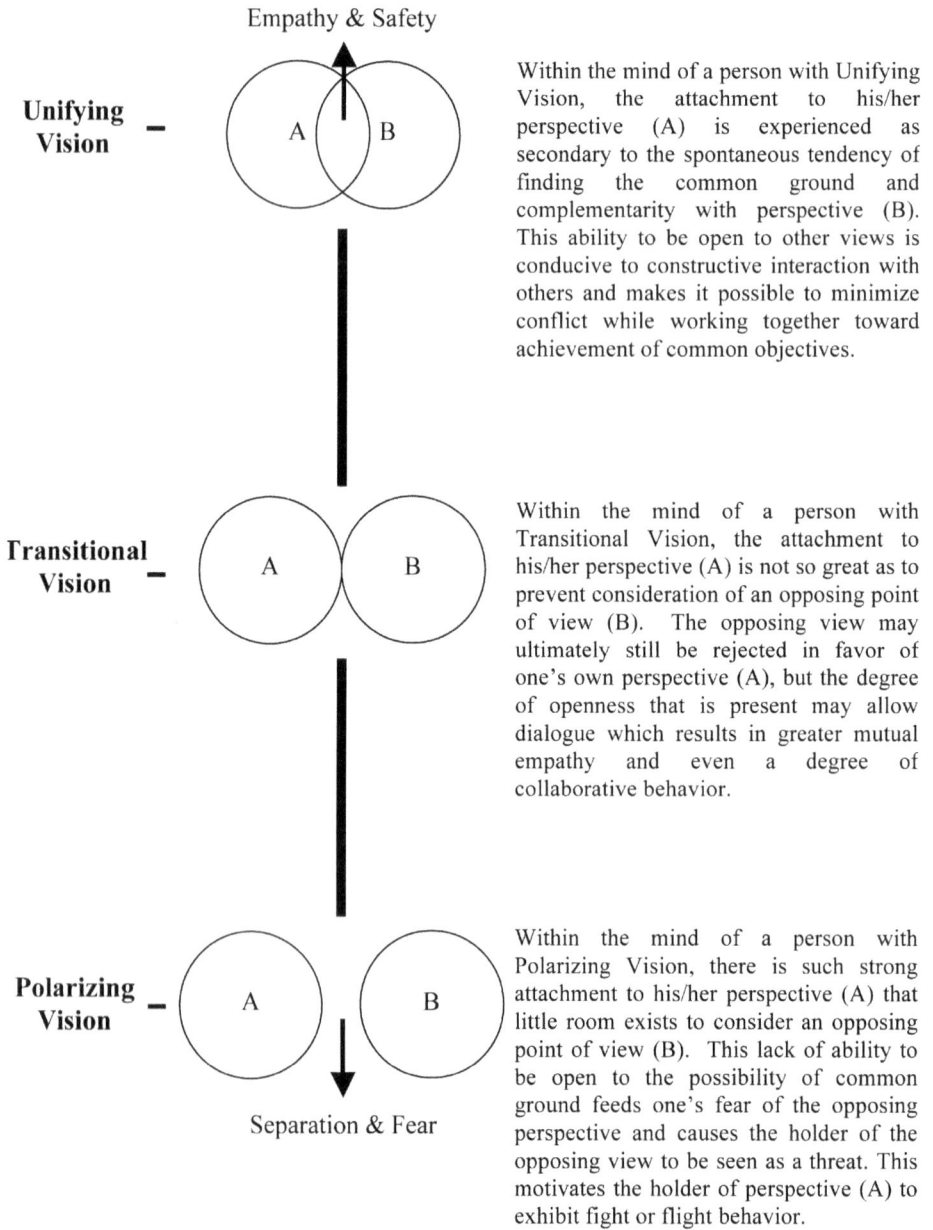

Empathy & Safety

**Unifying
Vision** —

Within the mind of a person with Unifying Vision, the attachment to his/her perspective (A) is experienced as secondary to the spontaneous tendency of finding the common ground and complementarity with perspective (B). This ability to be open to other views is conducive to constructive interaction with others and makes it possible to minimize conflict while working together toward achievement of common objectives.

**Transitional
Vision** —

Within the mind of a person with Transitional Vision, the attachment to his/her perspective (A) is not so great as to prevent consideration of an opposing point of view (B). The opposing view may ultimately still be rejected in favor of one's own perspective (A), but the degree of openness that is present may allow dialogue which results in greater mutual empathy and even a degree of collaborative behavior.

**Polarizing
Vision** —

Separation & Fear

Within the mind of a person with Polarizing Vision, there is such strong attachment to his/her perspective (A) that little room exists to consider an opposing point of view (B). This lack of ability to be open to the possibility of common ground feeds one's fear of the opposing perspective and causes the holder of the opposing view to be seen as a threat. This motivates the holder of perspective (A) to exhibit fight or flight behavior.

Figure 26.

Discussion of the three indicated cognitive frameworks reveals how the "glasses" through which an issue is viewed determine a person's perspective on the issue and his/her stance toward one holding an opposing perspective. These points are concretely demonstrated in the following examples. The views expressed in the examples do not represent those of the author or any specific real-life characters. They are presented merely to illustrate the kinds of variations in perspective that arise from different cognitive frameworks. As in figure 26, circles A and B are intended to represent opposite perspectives on the same issue:

Polarizing Vision   **Transitional Vision**   **Unifying Vision**

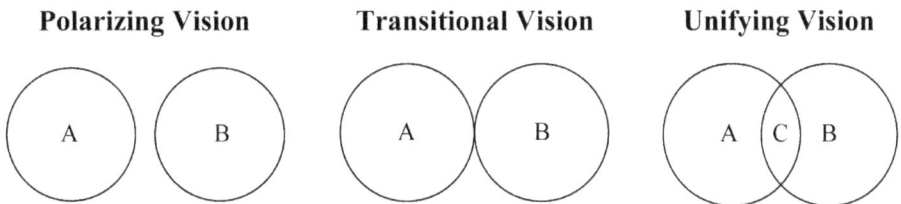

Extent of Government

One current, hotly-debated issue regards the extent to which government should be involved in matters that affect the citizenry. An individual dominated by *Polarizing Vision* will tend to gravitate to one or the other extreme of the issue, either believing that (A) government should have a strong role and prescribe policy in all areas of life, or that (B) government should have little or no involvement in anything. Such an individual will hold his/her chosen perspective with a high degree of conviction and use aggressive efforts to justify his/her view and/or convince others to adopt the chosen perspective.

The person with *Transitional Vision* will generally tend toward one side of the issue, but may be open to considering the validity of the opposing point of view. Additionally, the individual with *Transitional Vision* will tend to be less emotionally invested in justifying his/her position and/or convincing others to adopt the chosen perspective.

Instead of adhering exclusively to one perspective of the issue, the possessor of *Unifying Vision* naturally sees some validity to both sides (A and

B) of the debate and is inclined to craft the complementary parts of both extremes into a more inclusive view (C) that more fully addresses the issue as a whole. For instance, as regards the "extent of government" issue, a more *unified vision* might hold that government should become strongly involved in its response to an earthquake or other natural disaster, but less involved when the family or other societal structures have a situation under control.

Use of Force

Another commonly debated issue focuses on the interpersonal or international use of force to achieve an objective. An individual dominated by *Polarizing Vision* will tend to gravitate to one extreme of the issue, either believing that (A) force is never appropriate or that (B) force should generally be the response of choice, with a preference toward pre-emptive strike whenever possible. Such an individual will hold his/her chosen perspective with a high degree of conviction that may result in aggressive efforts aimed at justifying one's view and/or convincing others to adopt the chosen perspective.

The person with *Transitional Vision* will generally tend toward one side of the issue, but may be open to considering the validity of opposing points of view. Additionally, the individual with *Transitional Vision* will tend to be less emotionally invested in justifying his/her position and/or convincing others to adopt the chosen perspective.

Instead of clinging exclusively to one perspective of the issue, the possessor of *Unifying Vision* naturally sees some validity in both sides (A and B) of the debate and is inclined to craft the complementary parts of both extremes into a more inclusive view (C) that more fully addresses the issue as a whole. For instance, as regards the "the use of force" issue, a more *unified vision* might hold that force is appropriate in instances of self-defense or to combat tyranny, but inappropriate as a means of erasing or usurping the basic inalienable privileges of others.

Governmental Fiscal Policy

Another actively contested current issue revolves around governmental fiscal policy. An individual with *Polarizing Vision* will tend to gravitate to one extreme of the issue, either believing that (A) government should spend only when it does not create a deficit or require tax increases or that (B) government should spend whenever a compelling need arises, whether or not the reserves exist to cover the expenditures. Such a person will hold his/her chosen perspective with a high degree of conviction that may result in aggressive efforts aimed at justifying one's view and/or convincing others to adopt the chosen perspective.

The person with *Transitional Vision* will generally tend toward one side of the issue, but may be open to considering the validity of opposing points of view. Additionally, the individual with *Transitional Vision* will tend to be less emotionally invested in justifying his/her position and/or convincing others to adopt the chosen perspective.

Instead of holding exclusively to one perspective of the issue, the possessor of *Unifying Vision* naturally sees some validity to both sides (A and B) of the debate and is inclined to craft the complementary parts of both extremes into a more inclusive view (C) that more fully addresses the issue as a whole. For instance, as regards the "governmental fiscal policy" issue, a more *unified vision* might hold that government should generally only spend when the underlying financial reserves are present, but spend as necessary in the event of temporary emergencies related to national security or natural disasters, regardless of reserves.

Truthfulness

A philosophical and ethical debate has long existed around the issue of truthfulness. An individual with *Polarizing Vision* will tend to gravitate to one extreme of the issue, either believing that (A) one must always tell the truth or (B) one should tell the truth only when it conveniently suits one's ends to do so. Such a person will hold his/her chosen perspective with a high degree of conviction that may result in aggressive efforts aimed at justifying his/her view and/or convincing others to adopt the chosen perspective.

The person with *Transitional Vision* will generally tend toward one side of the issue, but may be open to considering the validity of opposing points of view. Additionally, the individual with *Transitional Vision* will tend to be less emotionally invested in justifying his/her position, and/or convincing others to adopt the chosen perspective.

Rather than adhering exclusively to one perspective of the issue, the possessor of *Unifying Vision* naturally sees some validity to both sides (A and B) of the debate and is inclined to craft the complementary parts of both extremes into a more inclusive view (C) that more fully addresses the issue as a whole. For instance, as regards the "truthfulness" issue, a more *unified vision* might hold that one should express the truth in all circumstances, except when others will be needlessly hurt with no redeeming benefit for anyone.

Suicide

Another commonly debated issue is suicide. An individual who "sees" with *Polarizing Vision* will tend to gravitate to one extreme of the issue, either believing that (A) suicide is never justified or that (B) self-termination is entirely an individual matter. Such an individual will hold his/her chosen perspective with a high degree of conviction that may result in aggressive efforts aimed at justifying one's view and/or convincing others to adopt the chosen perspective.

The person with *Transitional Vision* will generally tend toward one side of the issue, but may be open to considering the validity of opposing points of view. Additionally, the individual with *Transitional Vision* will tend to be less emotionally invested in justifying his/her position, and/or convincing others to adopt the chosen perspective.

Instead of adhering exclusively to one perspective of the issue, the possessor of *Unifying Vision* naturally sees some validity to both sides (A and B) of the debate, and is inclined to craft the complementary parts of both extremes into a more inclusive view (C) that more fully addresses the issue as a whole. For instance, as regards the "suicide" issue, a more *unified vision* might hold that under most conditions suicide is unacceptable, but that when consciously giving one's life so that another may live, or in cases of extreme and prolonged terminal illness, suicide could be an individual choice.

Pro-Life/Pro-Choice

A heated debate continues regarding termination of pregnancy. An individual who sees with *Polarizing Vision* will tend to gravitate to one extreme of the issue either believing that (A) abortion is murder and never appropriate or (B) the pregnant mother should have the exclusive choice regarding termination or continuation. Such a person will hold the chosen perspective with a high degree of conviction that may result in aggressive efforts aimed at justifying his/her view and/or convincing others to adopt the chosen perspective.

The person with *Transitional Vision* will generally tend toward one side of the issue, but may be open to considering the validity of opposing points of view. Additionally, the individual with Transitional Vision will tend to be less emotionally invested in justifying his/her position and/or convincing others to adopt the chosen perspective.

Rather than adhering exclusively to one perspective of the issue, the possessor of *Unifying Vision* naturally sees some validity to both sides (A and B) of the debate and is inclined to craft the complementary parts of both extremes into a more inclusive view (C) that more fully addresses the issue as a whole. For instance, as regards the abortion issue, a more *unified vision* might hold that pregnancy can be terminated when compelling health-related reason exists, so long as it can be done without injury to the mother.

The Origin of Greed

The principle subject of this book is economics and the achievement of the full wealth-generative potential of the global business sphere as a basis for funding the solution of our problems and the pursuit of progress. It is impractical to consider such possibilities without discussing greed, the behavior that threatens to derail pursuit of the common good in favor of excessive self-interest. For those in its grip, greed is easily justified by the need to guard against the uncertainties of life, the possibilities of sudden reversals of fortune, and the belief that others would take all for themselves in the face of limited supply. Fortunately not all individuals are possessed by greed. The greedy and generous share the same world, yet reach different conclusions about how to govern themselves. Gaining a perspective on what causes greed can help us make an objective decision about its appropriateness.

A person's view of the world is based on his/her cognitive framework. The view that justifies greed arises from a Polarizing Vision that lacks empathy for and feels separation from others. Such perception easily envisions an oppositional world of fragmentation, limitation, and insecurity that prevents one from seeing any underlying common ground with others. For those with a polarized perspective, greed appears justified.

But the root cause of greed is even more fundamental. The WGTSP principle states that although the parts of life may appear to some to be separate, they are ultimately integral components of a much greater whole. Those with Unifying Vision see this pervasive wholeness of life that dwarfs any sense of the limitation associated with a more fragmented view. Unifying Vision creates a sense that togetherness, completeness, safety and support-iveness are the basic nature of life itself. Examples exist of individuals with limited wherewithal who manage to feel contented and thankful for what they already have. In contrast, Polarizing Vision produces an experience of limitation, lack, and a sense of there not being enough; this causes greed, an insatiable hunger for more regardless of what is already possessed. As a result, already wealthy individuals sometimes pursue added riches to the expense of all other considerations, including health, harmony, legality, and care for the common good.

In this light, greed is an errant response to life, a mistaken understand-ing caused by seeing primarily the parts with no vision of the dimension that generates the greater whole. Polarizing Vision makes it difficult to see the fallacy in greed and the incompleteness of the world view upon which greed is based.

Alignment of Cognitive Frameworks with GEO

As is always the case, it is not the external phenomenon but the individual's cognitive framework that determines his/her view on a particular matter. Similarly a person's individual cognitive framework determines his/her alignment with a particular concept or model. As figure 27 indicates, the individuals with Unifying Vision, and to a lesser extent those with Transi-tional Vision, will most readily reject greed and embrace the concept and viability of Global Economic Optimization. Those with Polarizing Vision will be the least aligned with the GEO model, because GEO calls for a high degree of inter-firm coordination and cooperation within the world's industry segments. Such collaboration requires an absence of fear of the unfamiliar, an interest in understanding the perspectives of others, and a tendency to spontaneously seek the common ground or win/win approach in all situations. These characteristics are clearly held by those with Unifying Vision, within the reach of those with Transitional Vision, but not readily present in individuals with Polarizing Vision, who are unlikely to embrace the achievability of GEO, or feel safe enough to thoroughly consider the possibility of a win/win approach to business as a desirable and achievable

Alignment of Cognitive Frameworks with GEO

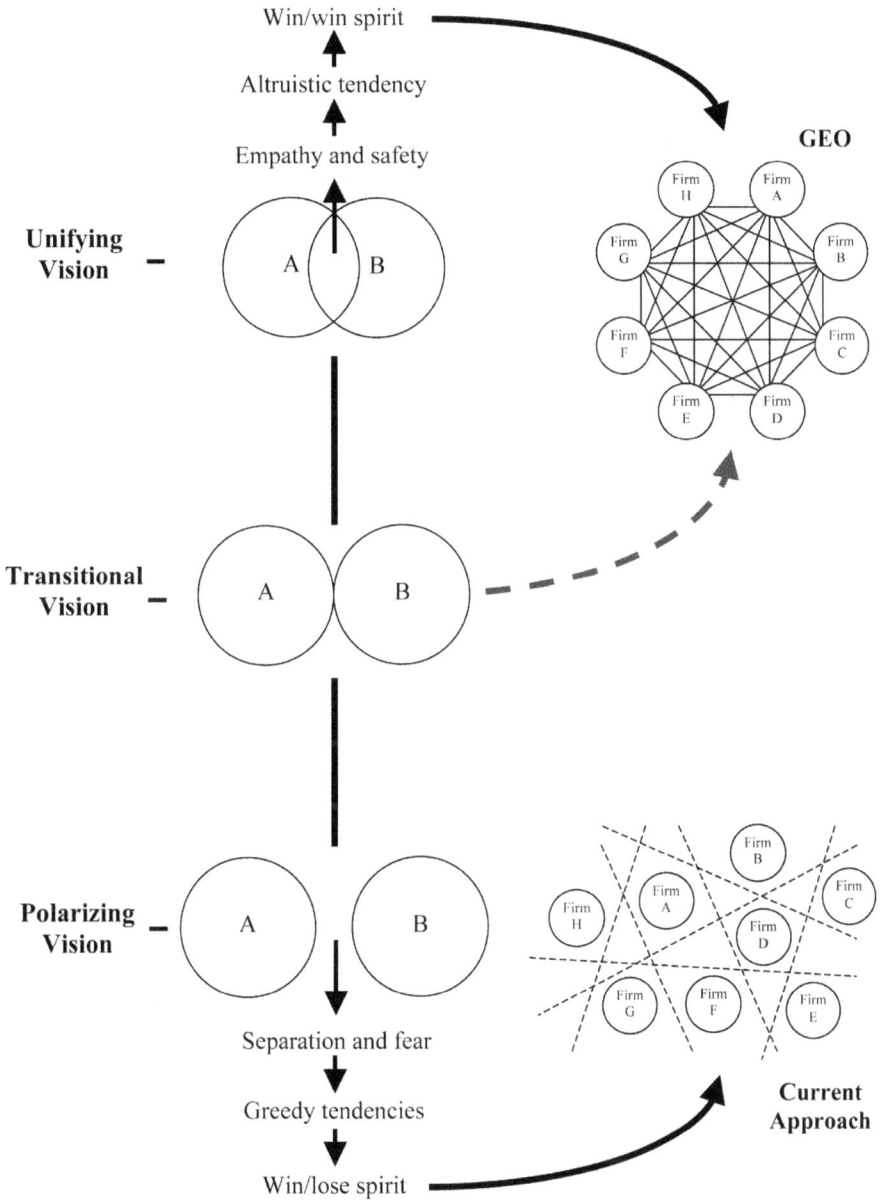

Figure 27.

alternative to the current win/loss approach of inter-firm competition that dominates the global business sphere.

Achievable Reality or Utopian Pipe Dream

This book has suggested that GEO's enabling foundation, the WGTSP principle, is so pervasive in life that its absence is far more the exception than the rule. Even those least likely to embrace GEO readily employ the WGTSP principle within a certain comfort zone. They begin to falter at the outer limit of their kindred group or "tribe" where they come into opposition with the "other". Examples of such discontinuous application of the WGTSP principle include the following.

- It appears among the players on an individual football team, but is not extended toward the opposing team.
- It is expressed within a family unit, but not as easily extended to non-family members.
- It is found within an individual religion but not readily extended to other religions.
- It is employed within a nation, but not among different nations.
- It is applied in the business sphere within individual firms, but not among firms throughout an industry segment.

It is an individual's cognitive framework that determines the extent to which he/she will feel safe enough to fully apply the WGTSP principle. Those with Unifying Vision and to some extent Transitional Vision are prone to be:

- individuals having strong friendships with players on opposing athletic teams
- individuals who feel as strong an allegiance to non-family members as to the members of their own family
- religious individuals who respect the beliefs of other religions
- individuals who are "global citizens" and owe their greater allegiance to mankind rather than a particular geo-political jurisdiction
- individuals who focus on achieving beneficial business objectives rather than preventing the success of others

Based on this, the achievability of GEO appears to be related to the degree to which mankind can adopt Unifying rather than Polarizing Vision. In a world riddled with conflict, greed, and diversity, what is the likelihood of mustering a viable consensus to adopt an approach like GEO that advocates the achievement of common objectives through pervasive coordination and cooperation?

Figure 28 demonstrates that the possibility of the adoption of GEO is greater than the surface appearance of things might suggest. Indeed, there

Potential Acceptance of GEO Based on Experience of the "Carrot and the Stick"

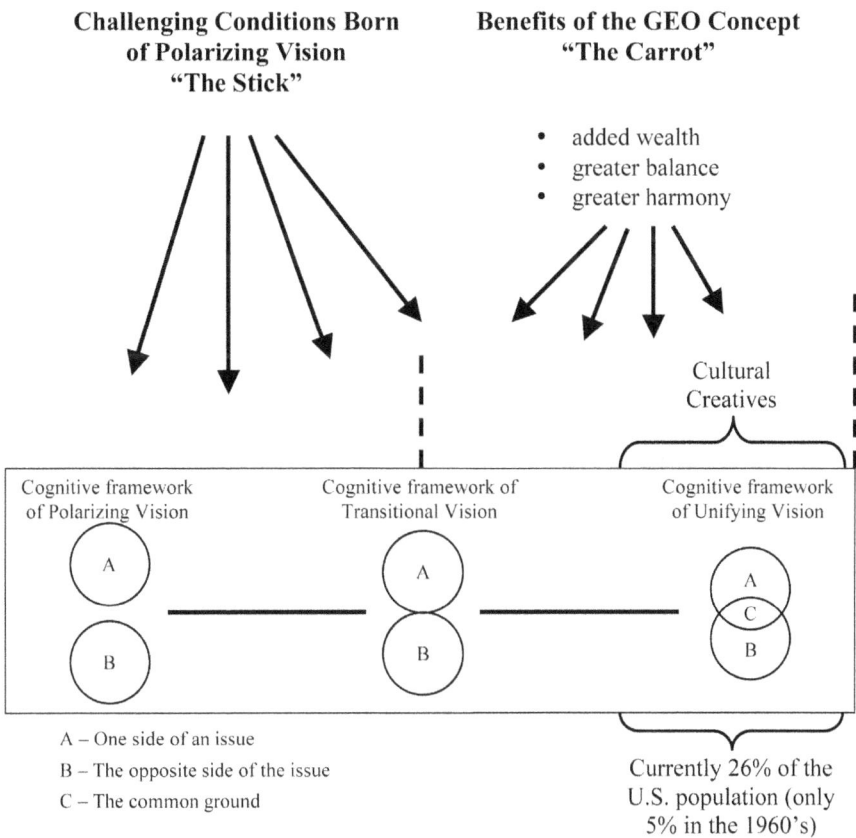

Figure 28.

is reason to believe that, given the right circumstances, the establishment of GEO is likely.

"The Carrot"

The preceding diagram illustrates that the ongoing influence of both the "carrot" and the "stick" will ultimately create an increasing desire for the implementation of GEO. As the GEO concept and its associated benefits of greater wealth, balance, and harmony ("carrot") gain favor among those who already have the "glasses" to appreciate the approach, a strong supportive group will emerge. Those who presently exhibit strong tendencies of Unifying Vision compatible with the GEO concept are known as the Cultural Creatives. As a group, they have a holistic view of life and an interest in the health of the whole, interconnected system rather than only of its isolated parts.[95] Specifically, as this relates to business, the old, competition-based viewpoints no longer apply. Rather, industry segments are not seen as battlefields, but as ecosystems with complex relationships to be nurtured.[96] This perspective, an expression of Unifying Vision, will readily embrace the GEO concept that encourages full pursuit of inter-firm collaboration within each industry segment to achieve the full wealth-generative potential of the segment as a whole. The Cultural Creatives have additional relevant characteristics in common[97] as follows:

- a love of nature and deep concern about guarding against its destruction

- a strong awareness of planet-wide issues (i.e. climate change, poverty, overpopulation, etc.) and a desire to remedy them

- a desire to have politicians and governments spend more money on education, community programs, and sustainable ecological practices

- an optimistic view of the future

- a desire to be involved in creating a new and better way of life

- a concern about big business and the negative means they sometimes use to generate profits (i.e. including destroying the environment and exploiting poorer countries)

Many believe that Cultural Creatives presently include more than 26% of the U.S. population and 30-35% of Western Europe, and that their ranks are increasing annually[98], from 5% of the population in the 1960's to their present proportions[99]. Such demographics strongly suggest that a large segment of the population already exists that will be favorably disposed toward the GEO concept once it is presented to them. Also, added support for GEO, though not as frequent, may arise when the concept is presented to those with Transitional Vision.

"The Stick"

Mankind has caused the current state of our world. Because Polarizing Vision has dominated our thinking and behavior to this point, we have produced circumstances and conditions that reflect the separation, fear, greed, and fragmentation characteristic of a polarized view of life. Polarizing Vision innately conceives solutions that do not recognize the broad range of variables in a given situation, and therefore, creates even greater problems. The aggregate and cumulative effect of this behavior has escalated our serious problems from local, to regional, and finally to the catastrophically global proportions that were specifically discussed earlier.

Left unattended, these challenges will threaten our very existence. This threat represents the "stick" that the world is struggling with and is the consequence of our own past thoughts and actions. Only by mending our ways and adopting a more effective approach, can we eliminate the pain and suffering that promises to increase if we do not change. This dynamic urges us to abandon our inclination toward polarized vision and adopt a more unified vision of life that acknowledges a much broader range of the variables that impact us. Consequently, the "stick" will join with the "carrot" and produce the dual influences capable of further swelling the ranks of those who see with Unifying Vision. The power of the "stick" to motivate unification and teamwork was evidenced in the Allied victory of WWII that was galvanized by the threatening spread of imperialism and fascism, in the U.S.' eventual success with its space program that was spurred by an early Russian lead with Sputnik, and in the increased American solidarity in the wake of the terrorist attacks of 9-11.

In these examples, groups who faced shared adversity put their differences aside and worked together to avoid an undesirable outcome. But in each of these instances, a "tribal" aspect of one group firmly pitted against the threatening "other" was still present. The consequences of our collective use of Polarizing Vision, the "stick", are global-scale challenges that threaten all mankind. If we accept the challenge to adopt the more effective mode of problem solving offered by Unifying Vision, we will eliminate the "other" mindset within the family of mankind. Our ineffective, polarized view of the world is our greatest opponent. To adequately respond to the "stick", we must realize that the enemy to our survival is not the "other", but is instead within our own minds. Our fear of the "other" is born of a polarized vision of the world that prevents us from seeing that we are far more alike than different and potentially more complementary than oppositional.

The "stick" may not only motivate more individuals to see with Unifying Vision, but also create a powerful effect among the Cultural Creatives. Though they are 50 million people strong, the Cultural Creatives are probably exercising only a small degree of their potential to influence cultural change. While they share a pre-disposition toward Unifying Vision, they are, as yet, not aware of themselves as a unified group with a collective identity.[100] As a result, the Cultural Creatives are not exerting as much influence on society as they would if they had group awareness and coordinated their group to empower the all-inclusive economic, political, and socio-ecological solutions that arise spontaneously from their Unifying Vision. It is reasonable to assume that in the near future, an increased experience of the "stick" could spur a heightened recognition of the stakes and mobilize the Cultural Creatives to further coordinate their efforts to drive change in society.

As the threat of the "stick" increases, along with a growing awareness that our current approach is not working, more openness to alternative solutions is likely to arise. Under such circumstances, a more unified and mobilized group of Cultural Creatives will find it easier to gain support for the more effective solutions that arise from their Unifying Vision.

Circumstances that Favor the Adoption of GEO

The foregoing discussion implies circumstances that favor the adoption of GEO as follows:

- The basic concept and benefits of GEO must become popularly known among the Cultural Creatives who, as a group, are most likely to embrace the approach. They currently represent a large and growing contingent of the populations of the US and Western Europe. Further popularizing GEO to those with Transitional Vision will bring additional support.

- The increasing global consequences (the "stick") of our collective polarized view of the world will likely create a growing sense that the present political, economic, and socio-ecological approaches are not working. As a result, those with Transitional and Polarizing Vision may become increasingly open to alternative solutions and new ways of seeing things. As Unifying Vision becomes more recognized as the fertile ground for effective problem solving, the popularity of Unifying Vision may increase. This "conversion" effect will augment the ongoing increase in the ranks of the Cultural Creatives, who have already grown from 5% of the population in the 1960s to more than 25% in the year 2000. Even at the base rate, almost 50% of the population may express Cultural Creative tendencies by 2040.

- The "stick" may also serve to galvanize the social efficacy of the Cultural Creatives who, at present, lack awareness of their potential impact. At some point, the increasing consequences of our collective polarized view of the world may become so threatening that the Cultural Creatives coalesce as a group and move to implement the more inclusive solutions that flow naturally from their Unifying Vision. If this occurs concurrently with more overall receptivity to new political, economic, and socio-ecological approaches, support for adoption of GEO as a more balanced and harmonious means of generating the additional wealth required to fund the solutions could grow dramatically.

The Tipping Point

If the previously discussed circumstances occur, we will likely reach a tipping point[101] that will trigger a dramatic increase in support of the adoption of GEO. The Tipping Point phenomenon demonstrates how trends grow from inception to full-blown status. This same dynamic underlies the growth of a wide range of occurrences[102] such as epidemics, product fads, crime trends, ideas, messages, and even cognitive/ behavioral shifts. In such cases, the growth of a particular phenomenon progresses at a metered and predictable rate, until reaching a critical threshold of involvement. At that "tipping point" a sudden and dramatic increase of participation occurs that renders the trend effectively irreversible. Similarly, the progress toward adoption of GEO is likely to leap forward when the critical mass of Unifying Vision reaches the tipping point.

A Race Against Time

In light of the factors just discussed, GEO will likely be an achievable reality rather than a utopian pipe-dream given the right circumstances. However, the issue of timing is critical, as is indicated in figure 29. It is unclear how

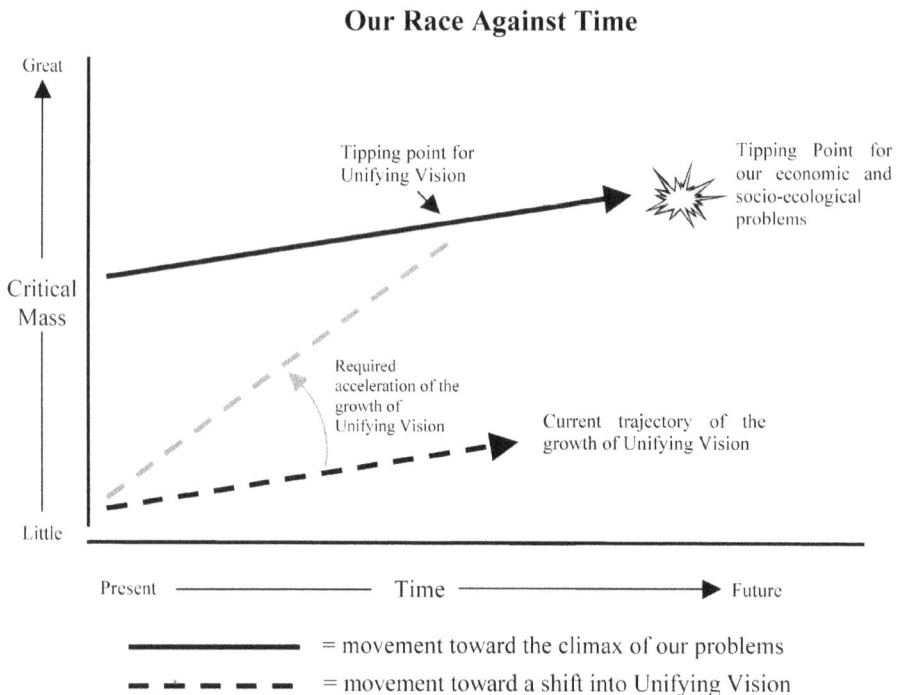

Our Race Against Time

Figure 29.

long it will take to reach the tipping point for Unifying Vision. Similarly, it is unknown how long it will take to reach the tipping point for the world's serious problems and suffer the dramatic increase and irreversibility of their negative effects.

Significant momentum is already building toward the tipping point of our economic and socio-ecological problems, but we are still at an early stage of the needed shift toward Unifying Vision. As a result, we must significantly accelerate our growth toward a more unified view. Mankind itself is the pivotal key to the outcome of this race. If we can shift quickly enough toward the use of the Unifying Vision with which GEO is aligned, we may be able to adopt the approach in time to generate the additional wealth needed to address our challenges and avoid the rapidly approaching tidal wave of economic and socio-ecological difficulties.

Pursuit of GEO Must be a Free Choice

Though time is of the essence with regard to our adoption of GEO, the decision to move forward must be completely voluntary and un-coerced. A significant effort must be made to educate all parties involved as to the nature and benefits of GEO, but the actual decision to move forward must be freely made by all parties. GEO will be able to generate vast additional wealth, but any use of intimidation or force will stifle cooperative spirit. While adoption of GEO is urgent, we must arrive at a broad-based agreement to do so achieved strictly by effective presentation of the benefits to be gained and the catastrophic consequences to be suffered if we fail to move forward.

Similarly, individual firms should not be mandated to participate in GEO. Even though coordination and cooperation will offer each firm the chance to be wealthier than through competition, some firms may choose to forgo the benefits of teamwork and go it alone. That will be their choice. However, if they make that choice, they will not only give up their share of the added wealth possible through collaboration, but also experience a significant operating cost disadvantage compared to those who chose to adopt GEO. A similar dynamic will occur in the various countries of the world. Some countries may choose to adopt GEO sooner than others, but the cost advantage and resulting benefits enjoyed by the countries that adopt

GEO will be a strong inducement for others to follow. So, even if GEO is adopted by some contingents sooner than by others, a built-in catalyst will ultimately draw hesitant parties to adopt this powerful approach for generating wealth while maximizing balance and harmony.

Chapter Twelve
The Bigger Picture

Amid the uncertainty of the present, we may feel that we have entered unfamiliar territory, without any precedents demonstrating how to move safely forward. While it may not be evident within a few short generations, history shows that over the longer span of time mankind has reached a similar position on numerous prior occasions. Within recorded history, many civilizations have come and gone. For example, British historian Arnold J. Toynbee identified more than 20 distinct past civilizations that progressed through the stages of birth, growth, and decay. Toynbee suggested that civilizations grow in response to challenge, with too little challenge leading to stagnation and too much challenge resulting in collapse. He believed that solutions to the civilization's challenges are developed by "Creative Minorities" and are then adopted and pursued by the dominant majority.[103]

Will our current global-scale challenges spur our civilization to greater heights, or will we crash and burn under the pressure of circumstances that exceed our ability to respond? The previous chapter suggested that our fate is largely in the hands of the Cultural Creatives, the present version of the Creative Minority to which Toynbee referred. But even if civilization as we know it crashes and burns, we can reasonably believe that mankind will continue on. As Toynbee observed, new civilizations arise from the ashes of the fallen, and to a greater or lesser extent, carry on the legacy of their predecessors.[104] Unifying Vision is the trait that can most effectively address our challenges and is therefore the legacy most likely to endure if this civilization falters. Unifying Vision embodies the most effective problem solving ability, and those with this more unified view are most likely to work through their challenges and move forward into the new order.

117

As the challenges born of Polarizing Vision increase, so does the potential for fear. But as Franklin Roosevelt said during the Great Depression, "the only thing we have to fear is fear itself—nameless, unreasoning, unjustified terror which paralyzes needed efforts to convert retreat into advance".[105]

Not the End, But the Beginning

Blinded by fear, we may have a tendency to miss the relevant bigger picture. While our problems could escalate and become irreversible when they reach their tipping points, it is not inevitable. The increasingly painful consequences of our polarized approach may provide the necessary impetus to re-create our lives on the basis of a more unified view of things. It is not without purpose that we face this situation. The inevitable changes it will spark promise to improve our human condition. As discussed previously, the "stick" that we are facing will naturally prod mankind to reject the dangerous use of Polarizing Vision and shift toward the more unified approach that offers greater balance and harmony to support survival and enhanced progress.

Managing Our Fears

Our present circumstance offers the possibility of a new beginning and an opportunity to both remedy our current problems and redo our lives individually and collectively through Unifying Vision. Knowing that a great potential lies before us, we have only to put our fears aside and embrace the opportunity at hand. Just as Roosevelt encouraged us to manage our fears of impoverishment, we must remain strong today so that we can stay focused on the path to our goal. If we recognize that fear is the real opponent, we will respond most effectively to the "stick" we are facing. Since our own Polarizing Vision has created the external problem, we must do the following:

1. Stop blaming our problems on anything other than our own ineffective polarized ways of viewing the world.

2. Know that our fears result from seeing through glasses that make us feel isolated and unable to find the common ground or bigger picture—This sense of separateness breeds uncertainty and

insecurity that, through psychological projection,[106] we project onto external circumstances that, in turn, become mistaken for the source of the fear.

3. While recognizing that specific external situations are not fear's source, experience our fears instead as mere emotions/sensations. This will disarm fear and give rise to the sense of presence and safety more characteristic of Unifying Vision.

4. Amid the experience of greater presence and safety, try to find the deeper meaning or bigger picture in the external situation—In a safer, more unified state of mind, we will be better able see more inclusive, balanced and harmonious solutions.

These practices will increase our ability to exercise Unifying Vision and to deal smoothly and effectively with the "stick" that we have collectively created. This approach is easiest for Cultural Creatives and within the grasp of those with Transitional Vision. Hopefully, those with Polarizing Vision will also be able to use this approach to navigate through the adversities before us, but their "glasses" may prevent them from easily disengaging from the belief that their external situation is the source of their fears and problems. But as the polarized approach to life becomes more apparently ineffective, its users will be increasingly prodded toward adopting Unifying Vision to solve their individual and collective problems.

A More Effective Basis for Solving Our Problems

Polarizing Vision tends to view the world as fragmented instead of interconnected and to see the sides of an issue as oppositional rather than complementary. One aspect of an issue is considered valid or important and all other perspectives are deemed mistaken or irrelevant. This blindness to potential complementarities makes Polarizing Vision an ineffective basis for problem solving. Figure 30, on the following page, illustrates the limitations inherent in employing a polarized view.

The example indicates that Polarizing Vision seeks solutions that select one benefit over an opposing one. Unifying Vision tends to, by its very nature, recognize the complementarities among the sides of an issue, and identify more inclusive and effective solutions.

An individual with Polarizing Vision will tend strongly toward one side or the other of a given issue. The example shown below considers the funding of progress and exercise of fiscal responsibility.

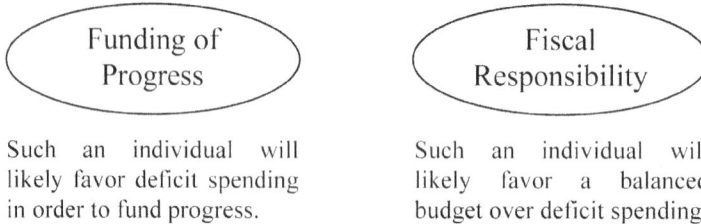

Such an individual will likely favor deficit spending in order to fund progress.

Such an individual will likely favor a balanced budget over deficit spending.

A strong preference for either funding of progress or fiscal responsibility will tend to inhibit formulation of a solution that embraces both positions simultaneously - funding of progress while balancing the budget - that could be pursued through an approach that creates additional wealth beyond current levels, making it possible to finance progress without deficit spending.

Figure 30.

Opportunity to Solve Our Problems and Recreate Our Lives

Unifying Vision is not only critical to appreciation and adoption of Global Economic Optimization, but also likely to spawn the solutions that GEO is meant to fund. The areas of conflict shown in figure 30 have been fertile ground for the multitude of problems that have long plagued us individually and collectively. Through the ages we have worked to eliminate our difficulties, but as Albert Einstein said, "Insanity is doing the same thing over and over again while expecting different results". What we have done again and again to no avail, is to see, think, and act from Polarizing Vision.

Chapter Eleven suggests that Polarizing Vision embraces a single point of view and refuses to consider other factors integral to an effective solution. Rather than employing inclusive approaches to problem solving, Polarizing Vision breeds both fear and an inability to empathize that obscures our view of the common ground and breeds conflict, hatred, persecution, exclusion, and violence.

A person consumed by Polarizing Vision is, by nature, unable to see the common ground, and is, therefore doomed to live in a constant state of fear and readiness to beat others to the punch. Polarizing Vision allows one to see only that which supports the belief that we live in a "dog-eat-dog" world. Our world will never change so long as we see through such "glasses".

Given the right circumstances, Unifying Vision will likely provide the direction that mankind desperately needs at this time. Figure 31 suggests that application of Unifying Vision to our age-old arenas of conflict will

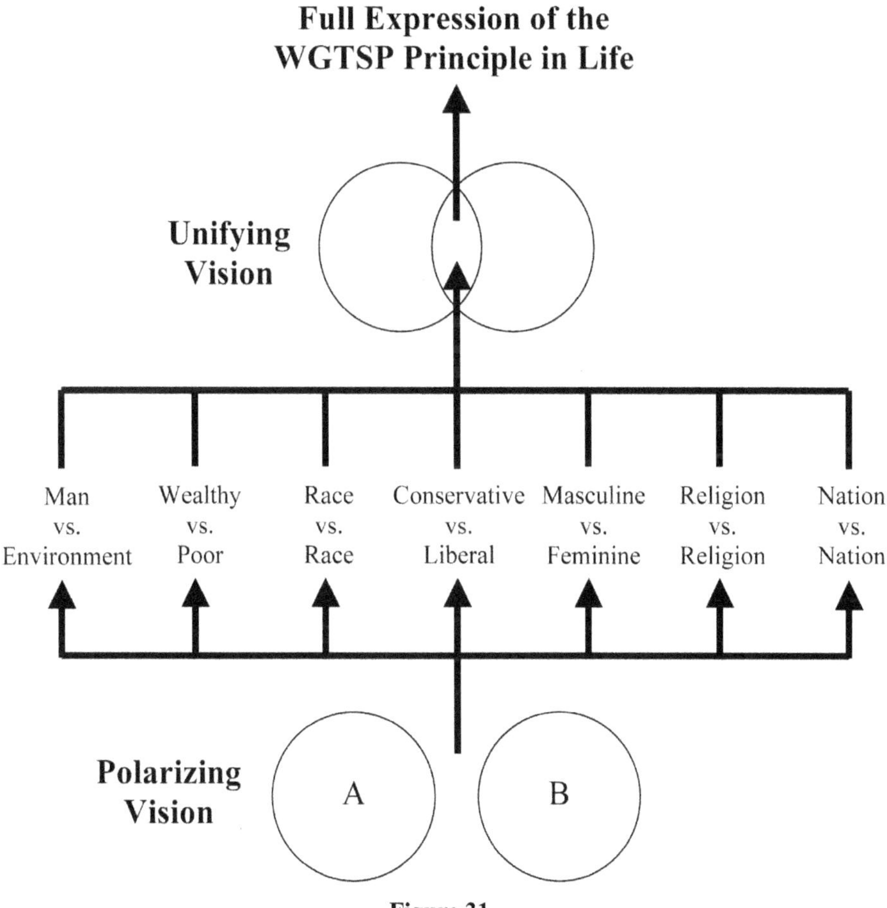

Figure 31.

result in new solutions. Our new unifying "glasses" will change our vision as follows:

- Where we felt fear, we will experience safety
- Where we misunderstood, we will empathize
- Where we saw differences, we will see the common ground
- Where we opposed, we will cooperate as a team
- Where victory necessitated defeat, there will be win/win outcomes

By merely implementing the solutions that flow spontaneously from our Unifying Vision, we will allow the full expression of the WGTSP principle that Polarizing Vision has thus far suppressed.

Although the conflicts in figure 31 have troubled mankind for thousands of years, these dangerous expressions of Polarizing Vision have been expanded to global proportions by the population explosion and technological advancements of the last hundred years. A shift to Unifying Vision will allow a natural selection of more effective problem solving as polarizing tendencies fall away. Seeing with and acting from Unifying Vision, we will find ways to minimize fear and conflict and to achieve not only greater survivability, but a whole in our lives that is far greater than the mere sum of its parts.

Chapter Thirteen
Key Questions and Answers Regarding Global Economic Optimization

While this book has discussed the key features of GEO, questions are surely to arise about such a unique approach and the magnitude of its intended mission. Therefore Chapter Thirteen will be devoted to addressing some of those questions that are likely to be posed.

What is Global Economic Optimization?

Our present global economic problems and rapidly approaching socio-ecological challenges require that we achieve the full wealth-generative potential of the global business sphere to remedy these difficulties. Due to the competitive dynamics of business that discourages firms from working together toward common objectives, we are substantially under-achieving our potential to create wealth. We need an adjustment to correct the situation. We will create vast additional wealth to address our challenges by infusing a high degree of inter-firm coordination and cooperation into each industry segment, but we must first realign the internal structure of each industry segment so that its firms are no longer pitted against one another. Then we can effectively pursue the many opportunities for inter-firm collaboration within the global business sphere. The result will generate several trillion dollars of additional wealth annually. These adjustments, along with the plan for distribution of the vast additional wealth, are what this book refers to as Global Economic Optimization, or GEO.

Is Global Economic Optimization an un-natural approach that will lead us into uncharted waters?

GEO is an example of the *whole being greater than the sum of its parts* (WGTSP), a phenomenon that occurs pervasively in many aspects of life. In fact it is hard to identify any phenomenon that does <u>not</u> express this principle. Consider the following list of instances where it is present:

- All atoms, molecules, and liquids, gases, and solids comprised of molecules
- All plants, animals (including humans), and minerals
- All manufactured equipment, machinery, devices, and gadgets
- All man-made systems and processes
- All multi-person or multi-component projects or endeavors
- All visual and auditory arts and commercial media
- All alphabet-based languages
- All personally, commercially, or industrially used objects that are comprised of more than one part
- All personal, familial, social, or professional pursuits that employ team work

Examples of the WGTSP principle are all around us. Many expressions of nature readily exhibit this tendency and, as creatures of nature, humans innately express the WGTSP principle as well. However, we are so accustomed to the phenomenon that we never stop to consider the special conditions that underlie it. In WGTSP expressions, the parts of a system work together to achieve the shared purpose. While the components each have their own purpose and integrity, their functions work in balance and in harmony with each other to support pursuit of the common good. Without the WGTSP principle, our world would be far less fruitful, balanced, and harmonious. One way to imagine how dysfunctional everything would be without it, is to examine the instances where we have intentionally suppressed the natural expression of the WGTSP principle. When we do so, less output, balance, and harmony result. In such instances, we have reached the edge of a comfort zone, where we have pulled back from collaborative interaction in favor of safety and security and, thus, sacrificed the WGTSP benefits. A prime example of this dynamic is the global business sphere where the inter-firm behavior of each industry segment is based on competition instead of collaboration. This "tribal" approach that pits firm against firm, sacrifices much of industry's wealth-generative potential that, globally, could amount to many trillions of dollars of additional wealth annually. Ironically, the WGTSP principle is rigorously applied within individual firms as they marshal their various departments, resources, and capabilities around the shared mission and strategy to maximize their income. We do this by natural inclination. GEO extends this same WGTSP principle beyond individual firms into the inter-firm dynamics of the world's industry segments.

Some may shy away from GEO fearing such broad-based collaboration, but the WGTSP principle that enables it is already so pervasive and spontaneous in life that it can hardly be considered unnatural or uncharted. Life validates the GEO concept and its benefits over and over again.

Is Global Economic Optimization an unachievable, utopian pipe dream?

The countless expressions of the WGTSP phenomenon in life include numerous examples of team work in human behavior. GEO is based on the same underlying principle. Because many individuals already consider it a viable approach, it is unreasonable to label GEO as an unachievable utopian pipe dream, yet many individuals may see GEO as an unrealistic fantasy. Chapter Eleven suggests that the approach is, in fact, achievable, but various individuals' cognitive frameworks will define GEO as either possible or completely unrealistic. Since GEO calls for heightened inter-firm collaboration within each industry segment of the global business sphere, those whose vision is inclined toward seeing the common ground between opposing views will believe GEO is desirable and achievable. Chapter Eleven referred to this mind-set as *Unifying Vision*. Those with *Polarizing Vision* focus mainly on differences and conflicts and those with *Transitional Vision* can sometimes find the common ground.

Many individuals with Unifying Vision and some with Transitional Vision will see GEO as achievable, while some with Transitional Vision and many with Polarizing Vision will see it as a pipe dream and possibly even undesirable. Presently, nearly 50 million individuals in the US possess tendencies toward Unifying Vision. These *Cultural Creatives* who currently represent a quarter of the population, numbered only 5 % in the 1960's. Their rapid growth implies that their ranks could swell to significantly greater proportions in the coming years. They presently see themselves as a much smaller contingent of the US population than they actually are. If they develop a valid group awareness, they will be able to exert themselves optimally as a unified force for positive change, such as toward GEO. If their ranks continue to swell at the current rate, and if the increasing need for wealth maximization, balance, and harmony drives them to unite their efforts, a tipping point could be reached that would create a widespread desire for the adoption of GEO.

This sort of powerful influence by a smaller group on the larger population is not without precedent. According to British historian Arnold J. Toynbee, civilizations seem to move forward as a result of the *creative minority's* response to the challenges of their time. Their creative solutions are subsequently adopted by the dominant majority, and life goes on. It now appears that the *Cultural Creatives*, with their ability to see the common ground, stand poised to create more inclusive/accretive solutions than those initiatives conceived under the influence of Polarizing Vision.

What makes such a large-scale change like GEO worth the considerable effort that will be required?

The inter-firm coordination and cooperation proposed by GEO will annually generate several trillion dollars of additional wealth, enough to solve the world's economic and socio-ecological difficulties and fund the development of the technologies, products, and services of the future. Without effectively meeting these needs, our long-term survival and progress in life is dangerously uncertain. This alone makes the required changes worth pursuing with appropriate urgency.

Our present business approach ignores the fact that inter-firm coordination and collaboration can create a magnitude of wealth that is substantially greater than the mere sum of each firm's individual results. Continued disregard of this opportunity will exact a heavy price by preventing the generation of enough wealth to fund the costs of survival and continued progress in life.

Why should firms adopt a more coordinated and cooperative approach rather than remain competitive?

By working together, the firms in each industry segment will generate enough additional wealth to fund both the solutions to the world's serious economic and socio-ecological problems and the development of the technologies, products, and services of the future. The business sphere can spearhead an epic-scale heroic initiative. This is, without question, sufficient reason for firms to participate. But, the business sphere is the bastion of profit orientation and entrepreneurial spirit. Therefore, the potential for businesses to become richer through GEO should also motivate them. As additional incentive, individual business people will receive special financial rewards when their efforts significantly contribute to maximizing the wealth-generative potential of their industry segments.

Many firms will embrace GEO as an opportunity to contribute strongly to the common good and maximize their own wealth-generative potentials at the same time.

How can we expect a paradigm shift of the magnitude of GEO to occur in any reasonable amount of time?

The present business paradigm is based on a win/loss dynamics where the success of one firm comes at the expense of another. Most of us are so used to this current approach that another way does not even occur to us. For an alternative approach to be considered seriously, its benefits must be overwhelmingly obvious, or the existing paradigm must no longer meet current needs. Both of these conditions clearly exist today.

GEO will annually generate several trillion dollars of additional wealth to solve the world's serious problems and to develop the technologies, products, and services of the future. Plus, the infusion of a win/win dynamic into the global business sphere will enhance our ability to work together toward accomplishing our shared objectives in spite of philosophical, religious, cultural, political, and national differences.

The proposed new paradigm not only offers the promise of overwhelmingly positive benefits, but can also effectively replace the existing approach that is rapidly losing its effectiveness in our current circumstances. The present competitive dynamics of the global business sphere are incapable of generating enough wealth to address our economic and socio-ecological challenges, many of which the existing approach has actually aggravated. The longer these problems go unattended, the closer we come to their tipping points where the escalation of difficulties and their potential irreversibility await us.

Though a widespread movement toward adoption of a new paradigm is not currently present, interest in GEO can be expected to swell as its benefits become widely known and as the world's unaddressed problems continue to grow.

Will the implementation of GEO be too large and complex an undertaking to be practically achievable?

Implementation of GEO will require a significant adjustment to the way the global business sphere currently functions. The most critical aspect is an adjustment in the largely polarizing way we view the world currently, with the business sphere operating on a competitive win/loss basis. This mind-set considers the proposed changes to be far more formidable than they actually are, and perhaps even unwarranted. However, viewed with a more unifying win/win perspective, the required adjustments appear less daunting and better able to meet our present day situation—a world that is too interactive and densely populated to tolerate an uncoordinated and non-collaborative win/loss approach to business.

The acceptance of GEO will likely seem most possible when our current insufficiently-addressed problems escalate. At that point, we will have no alternative but to raise the necessary funds at a magnitude that only a more holistic win/win approach in the business sphere can accomplish.

When future generations ask why we did not implement the solutions to our problems soon enough to prevent their cataclysmic conclusions, can we claim that the solution required too much effort? Hopefully, we will act proactively to adopt GEO and generate the needed wealth soon enough to avoid having to explain to our children why we stopped short of doing everything possible to ensure our survival and progress in life.

Why can we not just rely on the enhanced performance of individual firms to generate enough wealth to address the world's challenges?

The world is facing overwhelmingly serious economic and socio-ecological difficulties. We will probably be unable to generate enough additional wealth to solve these problems simply through improved performance by the individual firms in the industry segment. While an individual firm might increase its sales, it does so at the expense of other firms in the segment. Consequently, little <u>additional</u> wealth is created for the segment at large; it is only redistributed from the losers to the winners. Because of the typically slow rate of market growth, especially in tighter economic conditions, the only way to substantially increase the overall wealth being generated by an industry segment is to decrease the operating costs of individual firms while maintaining their sales volumes. Individual firms that are already adequately managed cannot dramatically decrease their operating costs without running the risk of becoming competitive losers in the current win/loss dynamics of the business sphere.

However, inter-firm collaboration can generate substantially more wealth than our current win, loss approach. The implementation of GEO can generate the significant additional wealth needed to effectively address the world's serious challenges.

GEO sounds like an advanced stage of business globalization that has previously benefited some, but created problems for many. How will GEO avoid such disadvantages?

Some believe that continued globalization has enabled large multinational firms to extend their influence in ways that sometimes work to the disadvantage of the larger portion of society.[107] Such individuals might worry that by increasing inter-firm coordination and cooperation, GEO will amplify the potential for such undesired consequences. However, the present win/loss dynamics of the global business sphere is the very dynamic that sometimes tempts firms to pursue profits to the exclusion of societal and environmental interests. By infusing business with a win/win approach, GEO will eliminate a significant motivation for excessive self-interest on the part of business that can disadvantage the masses. Also, substantial additional wealth will be created and designated to projects serving the common good.

Further, with GEO, each industry grouping will have a stated, segment-wide mission statement that calls for satisfying customer and socio-ecological interests in addition to maximizing wealth. A diverse team of professionals including industrialists, customer representatives, and environmental experts will manage each of the segment's firms. Therefore, decisions will be more aligned with socio-ecological interests, and will better avert the adverse side effects that have been attributed to globalization in the past.

How will we prevent the types of inter-firm collaboration that disadvantage the customers?

In the late 19th and early 20th centuries, the U.S. saw the rise of huge monopolies that were able to exert such great influence as to adversely impact employees, customers and competitors.[108] Regulations were enacted to break the monopolies and prevent the possibility of future uncontrolled concentrations of business clout. Today governmental agencies keep watch over the business sphere to ensure that competition is maximized so that customers suffer neither unfair pricing nor diminished choice of products/services.

Although competition obliges firms to practice fair pricing and to invest in product innovation, we pay a heavy price in the form of substantial stifling of the wealth-generative capacity of the global business sphere. GEO offers a better way to insure customer interests, one that does not deprive us of the vast additional wealth needed for today's economic problems and growing socio-ecological difficulties.

GEO will replace the current win/loss approach with the inter-firm coordination and collaboration that can annually generate trillions of dollars of additional wealth to fund solutions to our serious economic and socio-ecological problems. Unlike our historical experience with monopolies, this increased inter-firm cooperation will enhance rather than lessen regard for the interests of customers and society. The clearly stated mission of each industry segment will require a balance between wealth optimization and attention to customer and ecological interests. A team of industrialists, customer representatives, and environmental experts will manage each firm to ensure that decisions promote equitable pricing, product innovation, and socio-ecological sustainability. The mission statement will designate a significant portion of the added wealth generated through inter-firm collaboration to be used to fund development of the technologies, products, and services of the future. This, combined with the R&D funds already spent by each industry segment, will provide a greater emphasis on product/service innovation than with our current win/loss approach to business.

Finally, institution of a win/win approach to business eliminates a dynamic that may have helped to drive the previous destructive self-interest of past monopolies and today's multinational corporations. Enabling one firm to "win" without "defeating" another creates a new option that reduces the temptation to profit at the expense of employees, customers, society, and the environment.

***Competition motivates firms to achieve their highest levels
of excellence. Why should we remove this source of motivation
by replacing the present business dynamics with a win/win approach?***

The fear of being a loser motivates firms to push to exceed each others' capabilities and performance. In this sense, competition can drive business excellence. Many people simply enjoy competition—especially winning. Given that competition is functional and rewarding, what are the advantages of replacing it with an approach based on collaboration and a win/win dynamics?

Unfortunately, the win/loss dynamics of competition stifles the wealth-generative capacity of the global business sphere and annually deprives us of many trillions of dollars of additional wealth. Given the urgent need of funding the solutions to our economic and socio-ecological problems, this underachievement of our economic potential is unacceptable. By replacing our current approach with one like GEO that favors inter-firm coordination and collaboration, we can hope to correct the situation and generate the required additional wealth. This win/win approach will allow us to effectively compete against the world's problems which are far more formidable than typical inter-firm competitive dynamics. As a result, firms and their employees will be highly motivated toward excellence and enjoy the challenge of competing against global-scale problems that will require our utmost skill and resourcefulness.

How can we succeed in accomplishing grass-roots cooperation in
business when it runs counter to the idea that only the "fit" survive?

Some individuals who embrace the idea that only the "fit" deserve to survive, may believe that firms that win at the expense of others, become stronger in the process and ultimately strengthen the business sphere. But, many examples show that coordination and cooperation can achieve something greater. For example, tradesmen can coordinate their activities and cooperate to manifest the vision of an architect. Through teamwork, eleven offensive football players can score a touchdown. Through alignment with the corporate mission statement, the various departments in a firm can collaborate toward implementation of the business' objectives.

None of these initiatives would succeed by going it alone and losing the advantages of working together toward achievement of the greater accomplishment. Why, then, do we pit firms against each other when we could use coordination and collaboration to create vastly more wealth than the mere sum of their individual efforts? Even the strongest firm cannot generate the magnitude of wealth by itself that is achievable through collaboration with its peers. The choice is between less wealth and greater divisiveness on the one hand, and more wealth and greater unity on the other. Especially at this time of economic weakness and growing socio-ecological difficulties, we cannot afford to persist with the win/loss approach to business. The survival of the "fit" may be an observable phenomenon in nature, but it is misapplied in the field of business. This misapplication has justified competition where the strongest firms excel and the weakest fail. In reality the <u>one</u> firm may enjoy a gain, but the larger industry segment made up of many firms becomes weaker and fails to achieve its full wealth-generative potential. The lack of such substantial funds needed to effectively address serious economic and socio-ecological challenges threatens the world's safety. How can we continue to see the practice of competition as strengthening, when our current win/loss approach decreases our chances of survival?

Why not just raise the money to solve the world's
problems through some sort of corporate and individual tax?

Taxing individuals and organizations to fund solutions to the world's serious problems would be better than allowing our challenges to go unaddressed. However, despite the urgent need to solve these problems, increased taxes would further burden our already struggling economies. Taxes redistribute wealth rather than increase it. Only by increasing the magnitude of wealth flowing from the business sphere can we generate enough funding to solve the world's problems and not further damage the global economy. Infusion of coordination and cooperation in the global business sphere can generate vast additional wealth that our current win/loss approach cannot.

But more than funding solutions to the world's serious problems, GEO will also heighten our focus on development of the technologies, products, and services of the future and teach us how to work together toward achievement of our common objectives in spite of our philosophical, religious, cultural, political, and national differences. Such potential benefits make this proposed new approach, GEO, a better way to proceed than a program of tax increases.

Global Economic Optimization promises to generate the additional wealth needed to fund solutions to the world's serious problems, but some individuals already have adequate personal wherewithal to take care of themselves. Why should they care about the world's problems?

The Earth has grown so densely populated and so instantaneously interactive that any part of the world can rapidly influence every other part. Even the most affluent are subject to rapid reversals of fortune triggered by economic crisis, pandemic illness, violent conflict, etc. None of us can afford to ignore a situation in any area of the world where the seeds of such difficulties are germinating. Since no one can any longer escape the influence of the world's problems, we are left with no alternative but to proactively address these challenges at their epicenters.

Reversing the world's difficulties will require consistent large-scale funding, but individual, corporate, and governmental priorities prevented such funding even prior to our present economic malaise. GEO will be able to generate enough additional wealth to bolster the world economy and fund solutions to our serious socio-ecological problems.

Is GEO going to eliminate jobs?

The present win/loss nature of business discourages firms from coordinating and cooperating with each other to achieve maximum efficiency. Consequently, firms must each carry all necessary support functions rather than share common resources with each other. This saddles the business sphere with enormous redundancy, which includes human resources. Infusion of inter-firm coordination and collaboration will free up significant numbers of workers whose present jobs are redundant and, therefore, not really secure. Fortunately, with GEO, the world's redundant workers will not have to bear the angst of knowing that their employment is unnecessarily depriving the world of substantial wealth that might otherwise be used to address its serious challenges. GEO will create many new jobs for these workers as it eliminates the redundancies inherent in our present approach. The new jobs will support vital new initiatives which have not yet received the required attention. Some examples of such unaddressed pursuits that could employ many displaced workers are as follows:

- Development of sources of alternative energy
- Management of the effects of global climate change
- Response to impacts of extreme weather events
- Pollution control
- Elimination of abject poverty
- Population control
- Disease control in an increasingly densely populated world
- New infrastructure to mirror population growth and continued urbanization
- Repair/replacement of aging existing infrastructure
- Preservation/replenishment of fresh water supplies
- Preservation of ecological diversity
- Technology development for all of the above

These important initiatives can be pursued effectively with the newly available human resources and newly generated wealth created by GEO. The wealth will finance capital expenditures to equip the projects and to train and compensate workers staffing the initiatives. Since many of the staff will be coming from eliminated redundant jobs, re-training will be a key focus of the proposed approach.

Will participation in Global Economic Optimization be mandatory?

Participation in GEO will not be mandatory. This approach will require a high degree of inter-firm coordination and cooperation in the global business sphere. Therefore inspiration rather than coercion will be the key to spark cooperative spirit and collaborative activities. If firms are forced to cooperate, they will not likely be inspired to achieve optimum results; therefore, participation in GEO will not be mandated. The chance to generate enough added wealth to solve the world's problems as well as the opportunity to be richer than would otherwise be possible should make most firms enthusiastic about this new business approach, but participation will be their choice.

However, firms that choose not to join the effort may find it impossible to attain the efficiency levels of those firms that do choose to coordinate and collaborate with each other. These less efficient operations will have a hard time generating even their previous levels of wealth.

Why is Global Economic Optimization considered to be a win/win proposition?

GEO is a win/win proposition because it relies on firms' intra-segment coordination and cooperation rather than their pursuit of success at each other's expense. Firms will simultaneously increase each others' wealth more than would be possible without collaboration, thus a win/win outcome for all involved.

Beyond becoming wealthier themselves, coordinated and collaborative firms will generate enough added wealth to fund solutions to the world's serious economic and socio-ecological problems. The business sphere, society at large, and the environment will all be the beneficiaries of this win/win proposition.

Will the role of government be expanded through Global Economic Optimization?

GEO is not intended to be a governmental program. Governmental ownership or control of any of the world's firms will not be needed. Each of the world's industry segments will be a self-managing entity whose decision making aligns with a segment-wide mission statement. With GEO, voluntary inter-firm coordination and collaboration are viewed positively, so government will no longer have responsibility for ensuring acceptable levels of competition. Government will be involved in enforcement of laws already in place related to business dealings and handling of funds. Government will generally endorse and support the objectives of GEO and encourage the business sphere to adopt the approach to most effectively uphold the best interests of society.

How does GEO compare to socialism, communism, and capitalism?

Socialism and, to a greater extent, communism intend to decrease and ultimately eliminate class differences[109], the gulf between the haves and have-nots. Their emphasis is more on creating class equality than on optimizing the wealth generative capacity of the global business sphere. In socialistic models, property and production assets are state owned[110] and economic planning is centralized[111]. Because planning and decision making is top down, even totalitarian in the extreme case, grass roots level input and initiative that is critical to optimization of business performance is stifled.[112]

The principal aim of capitalism, conversely, is to maximize freedom[113] for those who pursue optimization of individual firm profits. This emphasis on freedom can actually accentuate class distinctions unless it is mitigated by preventative regulation. Some cases of unbridled economic freedom have actually created undesirable side effects for society and the environment[114]. Although the pursuit of individual firm profits is capitalism's paramount goal, it makes no deliberate attempt to maximize the wealth-generative potential of the firm's industry segment as a whole. As a result, the gains of one firm come at the expense of another and little <u>additional</u> wealth is created beyond the mere sum of the profits of the industry segment's individual firms.

GEO differs from socialism, communism and capitalism in key respects and avoids the chief difficulties inherent in all three. Unlike socialism and communism GEO allows the private ownership of property and the means of production. This is appealing to those who are already propertied and significantly wealthy. Currently, the mere redistribution of wealth to achieve class equality seems impractical and would produce significant social upheaval. GEO will not redistribute the world's existing wealth, but create vast additional wealth while greatly mitigating the ills of society that capitalism can accentuate. Finally, individual firm self management together with the inter-firm coordination and collaboration provided by segment-wide mission statements, will not stifle the grass roots level input and initiative that bolsters business performance.

Is the potential for Global Economic Optimization
lessened by the shift of business from durable products
and traditional industry to more service-focused pursuits
that are achieved more easily through electronic commerce?

In *Revolutionary Wealth* Alvin and Heidi Toffler suggest that the world has been progressing through three steps of surplus wealth generation[115] as follows:

1. Hunting and gathering activities
2. Industrialization and the production of durable goods
3. Offering less tangible services such as financing, designing, planning, researching, etc.

The Toffler's propose that at a more macro level business is progressing from focusing predominantly on hunting and gathering, to industrialization, and finally, to service orientation although all three forms of wealth generation can exist simultaneously in the same society. More focus on service offerings will likely increase electronic commerce and reduce the production of traditional durable goods. Will such a transition diminish GEO's ability to generate vast additional wealth?

If this transition occurs, GEO will still be able to produce the required additional wealth. The applicability of GEO is greatest with numerous providers and high provider overhead costs. This general rule applies for durable goods or services. If a newly developing area of business has few providers and low overhead costs, the wealth-generative benefits of GEO could be lessened, but not eliminated altogether, as long as the new line of business is not a single-firm industry segment.

The global business sphere presently contains a few thousand industry segments that are characterized by numerous providers and significant provider overheads. The application of inter-firm coordination and cooperation to these segments will create vast additional wealth. Even if these areas of business are in the process of being replaced by new service-focused pursuits with few providers and low provider overheads, such a transition will take some time. After all, how soon will we be able to dispense with major appliances, transportation equipment, household linens, cosmetics, etc? The time to fund the solutions to the world's serious problems is <u>now</u> and for the immediate next few years. We need the additional wealth <u>now</u> to get us past this critical stage of adverse consequences issuing from our prior, uninformed tendencies toward excess and self-interest without adequate thought to their negative impact. Despite an economic transition as suggested by the Toffler's, GEO should be able to generate the financial surplus needed to address our economic and socio-ecological challenges and ensure progress in life.

Some individuals raise the issue of a growing trend toward Conscious Capitalism, an approach to business that embraces higher ethical standards and genuine concern for the common good. As this trend continues to grow, will it lessen the need to pursue Global Economic Optimization?

In *Megatrends 2010,* Patricia Aberdene cites a growing movement toward Conscious Capitalism which she portrays as a more socially conscious, holistically-oriented form of business that encourages a more bottom-up versus top-down management approach.[116] She indicates that the "Cultural Creatives" who make up more than 26% of the US population and 30% to 35% of Europeans possess attitudes that are predisposed toward this type of business behavior.[117] She points to research indicating that businesses employing Conscious Capitalism tend to have better financial performance than those pursuing traditional capitalism.[118] The characteristics of Conscious Capitalism she refers to are shared by GEO.[119] Is there any additional value to GEO beyond that already occurring with Conscious Capitalism? If not, why take on the challenge of shifting the global business paradigm from a win/loss to a win/win approach?

While the underlying predispositions of the two approaches are highly compatible, GEO offers an enormous additional benefit. Conscious Capitalism calls for a more humane approach to business, but <u>not</u> for the adoption of pervasive inter-firm coordination and collaboration. The competitive win/loss dynamics prevalent in the global business sphere dictate that firms must excel at the expense of others, especially within the many markets still experiencing economic malaise. Conscious Capitalism maintains this same dynamic, so it will <u>not</u> generate as much additional wealth as the win/win approach. By instituting the win/win approach, GEO <u>will</u> allow the generation of the necessary vast additional wealth, clearly a supremely important purpose Conscious capitalism fails to address.

Since the Cultural Creatives also embrace the principles and objectives that underlie GEO, they will probably lead the shift away from the existing business paradigm to the win/win approach once they realize the highly significant additional benefits of GEO.

Some individuals believe we should adopt an approach referred to as participatory economics or economic democracy. Would implementation of such models eliminate the need for Global Economic Optimization?

Within the last decade several books have been written about the general economic approach called participatory economics or economic democracy. Among these works are *Economic Justice and Democracy* and *Panic Rules* by Robin Hahnel, *Parecon* by Michael Albert, and *After Capitalism* by David Schweickart. Key elements advocated by these authors are as follows:

- an extension and deepening of input into workplace decision-making for those impacted by such decisions[120]
- greater equity in the factors that govern payment for work performed[121]
- greater equity in the economic dealings among countries[122]
- alignment of supply and demand through participatory planning to avoid reliance on capitalism's free market dynamics to establish pricing[123]

These individual initiatives are cited as the adjustments needed to move us beyond our current form of capitalism and to an economic approach that is optimally fair and participatory and less prone to damaging society or the ecology.

Like this model, GEO is designed to support socio-ecological interests, but it will also generate the enormous additional wealth to fund solutions to the world's serious problems. Unfunded, these problems continue to move closer to their tipping points of irreversibility. We must keep these economic and socio-ecological difficulties from reaching such cataclysmic conclusions. The primary emphasis of GEO is to maximize the wealth-generative capacity of the global business sphere; secondary is the establishment of full grass-roots level participation in economic decision making. Maximum generation of wealth will require establishment of inter-firm coordination and collaboration throughout the global business sphere. This will require some degree of centralized planning, though still at a somewhat decentralized level, that will limit true grass roots level participation.

While GEO can eliminate abject poverty in the world, it will not focus on creating equity in people's earnings. Though pay equity may be universally agreed to someday, expecting it in the short term is probably not realistic. We must pursue maximization of wealth-generation as soon as possible.

GEO would be more likely to achieve world-scale economic, societal, and ecological benefit faster than participatory economics or economic democracy. Once the world's serious problems have been effectively addressed to ensure forward progress in life, approaches like participatory economics or economic democracy will most certainly provide the greatest level of participation for the largest number of people in the world. Because of GEO's emphasis on global scale inter-firm coordination and cooperation, it will help pave the way for world acceptance of some form of participatory economics.

Many individuals believe that some practices of big business have caused socio-economic damage. Can we prevent an even greater incidence of this under Global Economic Optimization?

The present win/loss dynamics of the global business sphere creates a "dog-eat-dog" situation in which competing firms work aggressively against each other to achieve maximum profits for stakeholders. Firms are even tempted to seek bottom line results at the expense of employees, customers, society at large, and the environment.

GEO will eliminate these temptations. Its new win/win dynamics will encourage previously competing firms to coordinate and collaborate to produce greater wealth for all firms, rather than compete for success at the expense of others. A team of industrialists, customer representatives, and environmental specialists, who work to achieve balanced decision-making that does not exploit employees, customers, society, or the environment, will manage each firm. Each firm's management team will align its initiatives with the segment-wide mission statement that requires inter-firm activities to both maximize wealth generation and uphold customer and socio-ecological interests. GEO will decrease the incidence of socio-ecological damage that currently exists under the win/loss approach.

Is there anything about Global Economic Optimization that can be considered un-American or counter to inalienable human rights?

Determining what is un-American and what is not is difficult because the United States is comprised of such diverse people and ideas. This unique diversity and its welcome co-existence embody the spirit of America. This country has enduringly cherished some important ideals since its founding as follows:

- Life
- Liberty
- Pursuit of happiness
- Innate equality of all people
- Opportunity for the governed to have an impact

The implementation of GEO will move each of these ideals closer to fulfillment.

Life

Generating the vast additional wealth needed to solve the world's serious problems and ensure ongoing progress in life will effectively eliminate daily concerns about the large-scale loss of life and property that will likely accompany an unchecked escalation of economic and socio-ecological difficulties. GEO will preserve life for many more than would otherwise be the case.

Liberty and the Pursuit of Happiness

GEO will preserve life and effectively address our serious problems creating a greater sense of safety and an ongoing growth of prosperity. Many more people will more easily pursue happiness. With the absence of the serious problems that currently threaten us, government or powerful individuals will not need to push for adjustments to our civil liberties in the name of protecting us from the dangers that might require would-be protectors to have enhanced authority.

Innate Equality of All People

By generating funds to address our challenges, GEO acknowledges that the opportunity to pursue a good life should be available to all people, not just the rich and powerful who currently are better able to structure their personal circumstances to be less susceptible to economic and socio-ecological difficulties. Simultaneously, this new approach acknowledges individuals' rights to the wealth and power that good fortune grants them. GEO does not take from the rich to give to the poor, like Communism and other socialistic ideologies. Rather, it offers the opportunity to generate vastly more wealth than our present economic approach to ensure the equality of all and the right of anyone to pursue life's bounty.

Opportunity for the Governed to Have an Impact

Finally, the proposed governance of this new approach will enormously empower society to influence the success of GEO. Both the progress of the business sphere and the application of the funds to our world's problems will be highly transparent. Society's role will be to watch the process and oversee accountability on the part of business. This will increase society's authoritative role in issues that impact us. In our present forms of democracy, legislative and executive branches of government make decisions on behalf of the people. While the complexity and diversity of issues in life may require a class of proxies representing the interests of the masses, it still produces a sense of disengagement and disempowerment. GEO will encompass ranges of issues narrow enough to allow the public more direct monitoring. The following issues will be tracked:

- Is maximization of wealth being achieved?
- Are customer interests being upheld?
- Are the interests of society and the ecology being pursued?

The results will be tracked and published for all to see simultaneously. This information will empower the people with knowledge of both the good and bad news. Considering our escalating problems, the masses will be keenly interested in ensuring that these issues are being addressed effectively. This more direct role will give the masses a new, more active place in the democratic process that is likely to "creep" into other areas of life that would benefit from grass-roots level participation.

Global Economic Optimization is a big undertaking that needs to be discussed thoroughly in advance of any decision to move forward. Are our challenges really threatening enough to warrant such an approach? If so, does some other way exist to generate the funds needed to solve our problems?

Do we need to experience additional economic and socio-ecological deterioration before we are motivated to act? Only time will reveal the full magnitude of the situation, but evidence continues to show that our problems are progressing and approaching their tipping points. Allowing the tipping points to draw nearer just to assure ourselves of a reason to act, is like playing Russian roulette. Ultimately, overestimating the problems or over-engineering the solutions will be better than doing too little too late. Assuming a real reason to act and/or the wisdom of erring on the side of safety, let us consider if there is a better approach than GEO to generate the funds needed to effectively address the world's challenges.

Rather than embark on a detailed examination of all possible ways of obtaining funds, let us focus on a more basic level of the issue. Fundamentally, only two approaches will be able to generate the vast funds needed to solve the world's serious problems. Either we generate additional wealth beyond the current levels, or we redistribute the wealth presently being produced. To avoiding "robbing Peter to pay Paul", we must generate additional wealth.

Our present win/loss approach generates wealth from the business sphere that is only the sum of what each firm produces individually. A win/win approach to business like GEO will create inter-firm coordination and cooperation allowing the generation of vast additional wealth far beyond the aggregate results of the individual firms. This creation of a whole which is greater than the sum of its parts is necessary to generate the magnitude of additional wealth to effectively address our serious challenges. This is the focus of GEO. Such unique focus distinguishes it from other options that involve wealth redistribution which will require us to make the hard choices between what gets attention and what goes unattended. GEO will generate enough funds to move forward on all necessary fronts simultaneously.

What if GEO is established as the new paradigm and it falls into the hands of those who would use it for personal gain at the expense of the masses?

GEO proposes that a coordinated and collaborative business sphere be used to fund solutions to the world's serious problems, set mankind on the path of maximum progress, and otherwise benefit the entire population of the world. Could GEO's highly integrative approach be abused by those who might seek to enrich and empower themselves at the expense of the masses? The current, less-integrated approach to business has already produced some degree of such abuse.[124] Could greater damage be created by the abuse of GEO?

This valid concern deserves serious consideration. To do so we need to weigh the magnitude of the consequences we will face by staying our present course, against the likelihood of the misuse of a maximally integrated global business sphere.

The introduction to this book presented the economic and socio-ecological challenges that may alone or collectively reach their tipping points of dramatic escalation and/or irreversibility. The consequence may well be catastrophic, challenging our very survival and progress in life. Only adequate funding of the solutions to our problems can keep us from the brink of disaster. Coordination and cooperation in the global business sphere will deliver enough additional wealth to do this. Simply put, we may not survive unless we achieve the benefits of GEO.

The thought of full-blown global economic collapse or socio-ecological destruction is terrifying. However, also frightening is the possibility that, despite good intentions, we might create a maximally-integrated global business sphere that comes under the control of those who would abuse it to serve their own interests at the expense of many others. Although possible, there are factors that make such an unintended reversal less than likely:

- In GEO, the grass roots-level mechanism for planning and decision-making is the self-managed team of each firm that operates within its corresponding industry segment. This all-pervading influence of self-management within the global business sphere will foster a psychology that is innately resistant to the urgings of an autocratic elite bent on self-interest at the expense of the masses. This mechanism of self-management is aligned with the relevant industry segment's mission statement that specifically holds that the planning and decisions of all firms will uphold the best interests of the customers, ecology, and society at large. Continual reference to this mission will foster a sense of purpose that is innately incompatible with the intent of anyone interested in instituting an agenda characterized by narrow self-interest.

- The proposed system for monitoring the generation, holding, distribution and use of the vast additional wealth generated through GEO provides complete transparency for the general public. This will, in turn, stimulate accountability from those who are infusing coordination and cooperation into the business sphere. This level of transparency and accountability will make it very difficult for anyone with selfish motives to assume any degree of control without immediately alerting the masses.

- Through GEO we will learn to put our philosophical, religious, cultural, political, and national differences aside and work effectively to achieve our shared objectives. We will experience the fullest meaning of the saying "united we stand, divided we fall", and our unity will deter any self-interested individuals from gaining control of the wealth-generative machinery by attempting to divide and conquer the masses.

- The masses would not be likely to knowingly choose a way of life that damages most and privileges a few. The attempts of a self-interested elite to implement such a negative agenda would almost certainly be based on promises of making things better. Such attempts are more appealing when general socio-economic conditions are poor. The more threatening our conditions, the more appealing the promises to those concerned most about their safety and security.[125] If GEO generates the needed funds and solves the world's economic and socio-ecological problems, proffered "rescues" will have less appeal. When safety and security are assured, self-interested autocrats are not likely to gain much foothold. Without GEO and the corresponding enhanced wealth generation, a very good chance remains that our problems will persist and worsen to the point where individual regions, perhaps the entire world, will genuinely need to be rescued. The proposed optimization of the wealth-generative capacity of the global business sphere, GEO can create a situation that is the least likely to empower self-interested autocratic groups or individuals.

In conclusion, not only are dire consequences likely to result if we do not pursue GEO, but the built-in dynamics of GEO would protect it from being exploited by a selfish few at the expense of the masses. Such abuse seems more likely if a concerted effort is not made to maximize the world's wealth and apply it for the common good.

Final Thoughts

This book has introduced Global Economic Optimization, a new, more balanced and harmonious concept capable of maximizing the wealth-generative capacity of the global business sphere. Pursuit of this model will annually result in trillions of dollars of additional wealth to bolster our economies and effectively address the world's rapidly approaching socio-ecological difficulties. But we can also expect the realization of other important benefits as follows:

- Development of the technologies, products, and services of the future

- Opportunity for individual firms to become richer than they possibly could without pursuit of this new approach

- Financial rewards for individuals whose achievements contribute substantially to accomplishment of this new approach

- Creation of meaningful new jobs for those currently occupying redundant positions

- Engendering a unifying influence that cuts across our philosophical, religious, cultural, political, and national differences

While many positive benefits can be gained through implementation of this new model, cataclysmic consequences may occur if we do not move forward. Without proper attention to their solutions, our economic and socio-ecological problems grow increasingly dangerous and move relentlessly toward their tipping points where sudden escalation and even irreversibility await.[126]

GEO may first appear to be a Utopian pipe dream, but it is based on the principle of the whole being greater than the mere sum of its parts. This phenomenon is so pervasive, that its absence in life is far more the exception than the rule. The exceptions that do exist in the man-made world arise from a "tribal" mentality that is the consequence of viewing the world through Polarizing Vision.

As relates to economic matters, Polarizing Vision causes us to believe that competition in the global business sphere is both necessary and beneficial. But through the "glasses" of Unifying Vision, competition is seen as a source of imbalance, disharmony, and under achievement of the wealth-generative potential of the global business sphere. Reflecting this view, GEO is both achievable and desirable. Acceptance or rejection of the concept is wholly dependent upon the "glasses" through which we view the world. If the majority sees the world through Unifying Vision, the desire for the adoption of GEO will be wide spread.

Although Polarizing Vision is the dominant approach for many of us, a significant portion of the population already employs a more unified view of life. Such individuals, collectively referred to as the Cultural Creatives, represent a quarter of the US population and a third of the inhabitants of Western Europe. The ranks of the Cultural Creatives are growing steadily, up from a mere 5% in the 1960s. Although they presently lack awareness of their size, they may soon galvanize in response to our accelerating challenges and exert a powerful influence toward adopting GEO.

Such circumstances could lead to solving the world's serious economic and socio-ecological problems, but we may run out of time if we reach the tipping point of our problems before we implement and experience the benefits of GEO. The result of reaching the tipping point will be catastrophic.

Initially, those with Polarizing Vision will not comfortably embrace GEO or grasp its viability. It becomes critical that those with a more unified view of life move forward with utmost sincerity, taking every opportunity to become anchored in Unifying Vision and to implement the innovative new solutions that arise from their more inclusive view of the world. In this way, everything possible will be done to achieve adoption of GEO before reaching the tipping point of our serious problems. For the sake of all future generations, let us not realize in retrospect, that we did too little too late.

Appendix A
Additional Reflections on Mastery of the Core Competencies Underlying Individual Business Performance

The suggested path for optimizing the performance of individual businesses was broadly outlined in Chapter Two of this book. Following are some additional thoughts regarding mastery of the three key core competencies upon which business success depends.

Identification and Management of the Core Business

Standards for best practice can be built on an already well established foundation in the identification and management of the business core. As is indicated in current literature, a business' core <u>must</u> be accurately identified. The forces of globalization, increased micro-segmentation of industry sectors, and re-defined traditional value chains[127] make this an increasingly difficult task. Yet with sharpened discrimination, we must establish the boundaries of the core business, including the understanding of both what is, and is not part of the core[128]. Boundaries must be categorized as stable or shifting. A clear understanding must be created of the true source of differentiation from the competition, and of where to make greatest profits now and in the future[129]. To have a fully empowering vision we must also understand the critical areas of adjacent activity, and the competitive landscape[130].

Once the core business has been effectively identified, we can set about to optimize its potential. Many businesses underestimate the value of their cores[131], so care must be taken to not set goals too low. To do so, would deprive the core of the focus and capital needed to optimize growth and profits and to invite the competition to capitalize on the under-exploited opportunity[132].

When considering the possibilities of the identified core, we must re-member the two most significant indicators of potential for high growth and profits as follows:

• Presence of a single strong core businesses versus a more diversified approach[133]
• Leadership position in the core business[134]

If one or both of these conditions are present, increased vigilance is needed to ensure that the business potential is not viewed too conservatively.

Since the core business is often under-optimized, care must be taken not to prematurely abandon the core to pursue growth in other areas. Pre-mature abandonment of the core results in loss of growth and profits in-stead of gain[135]. The more effective strategy is to use the solid core as a bridge for well-conceived expansions into adjacent areas of the business environment[136].

The preceding are some important findings that have surfaced from the research done on the subject of the business core and its management. As indicated earlier, further work is needed to create a full set of agreed upon best practices for business executives to systematically master.

Divestiture of Superfluous Assets, Resources, or Capabilities

We need to develop best practice regarding divestiture of non-core business components. These standards need to cover both the queuing up of the non-core components and use of the most effective means of divestiture. Fol-lowing are some useful ideas around which these standards may be built.

Identification of non-core elements will naturally occur as a result of effective core identification and management, but mechanisms need to be in place to ensure timely queuing up of the prospective divestitures. An in-dividual or team should be empowered in each business to encourage timely divestiture of non-core business components. This individual or team would ensure the following:

- Focus and investment is not diverted away from pursuit of the core.
- Proceeds from divestiture of non-core components are available for investment in the core as soon as possible.

In addition to ensuring that non-core business components are queued for timely divestiture, the standards for best practice should include guidelines on how to most effectively optimize divestiture proceeds, but this should not be the sole consideration. In any divestiture, an opportunity exists to select a buyer whose own core business will strongly benefit from the addition of the divested component. Simultaneous achievement of both outcomes is ideal because the overriding goal, as proposed in this book, is optimization of the wealth generative capacity of the global business sphere, instead of merely creating advantage for one at the expense of another.

Although the interests of the seller and buyer may seem naturally at odds, in this situation, they are perfectly aligned. The seller can more easily optimize proceeds if the non-core component is sold to a business whose own core needs the asset, resource, or capability in question. Such a buyer will be able to create maximum wealth from the component and, therefore, justify payment of a higher price.

Thus, it should be possible to maximize the proceeds from the acquirer who has the opportunity to create greatest wealth from the newly acquired component. No knowledgeable buyer would be willing to pay the seller the full value of the potential wealth to be created after the divested component has passed to the new owner, but it should be possible for the seller to obtain a reasonable premium over the stand alone value of the component. In this way, proceeds are optimized for the divested component that can subsequently produce optimum wealth in the hands of the right buyer.

This approach is employed most effectively with the assistance of a skilled advisor or intermediary. The dynamics of optimizing the proceeds are difficult to achieve successfully without a mediating influence, such as an advisor. The advisor must be adept at eliciting the buyer's highest reasonable price in relation to the wealth that the buyer may subsequently generate.

The preceding are some basic findings related to divestiture of non-core assets, resources, or capabilities. Again, further work should be done to create a full set of agreed upon best practices to be systematically mastered by business executives.

Effective Acquisition of Required Assets, Resources, or Capabilities

Best practice needs to be developed regarding acquisition of the business components needed to support effective pursuit of the core business. This is especially important because acquisitions frequently fail to create value. The standards of best practice should include guidelines for effective identification of the right components to acquire and the most effective means of securing the identified components.

Securing components is especially difficult to accomplish without a particularly adept intermediary, since even active sellers tend to view buyers as adversaries. Obtaining the appropriate intermediary is critical, but few of them are properly qualified. Still, optimum results are unlikely without such assistance.

Using best practices and with proper assistance, acquisitions can contribute greatly to the generation of wealth from the core business. If the acquirer's core is supplemented by the full range of needed assets, resources, and capabilities, the stage will be set to achieve the fullest optimization of the acquirer's business.

While the preceding are important considerations regarding the use of acquisitions to optimize the core business, some precautions should also be noted. First, care must be taken not to be distracted from the primary focus in hopes of using the core to generate added value. It is possible to create added value, but misalign one's business with the original core. This could deprive the core of resources and result in sub-optimized value.

Second, it is essential to stay focused on acquiring only the components needed for the pursuit of one's own business core. Often the most suitable components are entangled within other businesses that contain elements not usable by the buyer's core. If at all possible, the transaction should be structured so that the buyer obtains the desired component, but leaves all others with the seller.

If this is not possible, the buyer may continue to pursue the transaction if a certainty exists that the buyer can later sell the unwanted part. The transaction should not be pursued if the buyer cannot eliminate the undesirable components for an indefinite period following completion of the transaction. A possible exception is if no alternative way can be found to obtain the desired component, and the buyer can generate enough wealth from the desirable component to compensate for having to keep the undesirable components.

During the duration of the transaction, close scrutiny must be given to all factors and data that can effect subsequent generation of wealth by the buyer. Thorough identification must be made of all factors that might inhibit generating the anticipated wealth. An often underrated factor is the cultural and attitudinal differences that may exist between the buyer's and seller's people, but many other issues must also be carefully considered to determine if subsequent wealth generation is achievable. Individuals taking the lead in acquisition of needed assets, resources or capabilities should have appropriate subject knowledge of the issues involved and be held fully responsible for ensuring that the acquisition enhances the core's value.

Next, the buyer <u>must not</u> pay too much for the desired component. Acquisition should be pursued only if its combination with the buyer's core business creates enough wealth beyond the stand alone values of the two entities. The anticipated extra wealth must be confirmed during due diligence by examining the economic impact of adding the relevant assets, resources, or capabilities to the acquirer's core.

Before the acquisition is completed, an integration plan should be formulated. This plan must clearly outline the specific tasks and sequence of events to be pursued upon closing the transaction. The goal is to ensure not only retention of the stand alone value of the acquired component, but also rapid generation of the extra wealth contemplated by the combination of the core business and the acquired components. Once the transaction is complete, the integration plan must be pursued aggressively and according to the prescribed sequence in order to retain stand alone value while developing the extra wealth intended by the acquisition.

The preceding are some fundamental concepts that should be included in a complete set of standards related to acquisition of assets, resources, or capabilities needed for optimization of a business's core. As indicated earlier, further work should be done to create a full set of agreed upon best practices for business managers to systematically master.

Summary

This Appendix A has provided additional thoughts regarding the maximization of individual business performance through mastery of three key competencies as follows:

- Identification and management of the core business
- Divestiture of superfluous assets, resources, or capabilities
- Effective acquisition of required assets, resources, or capabilities

The intention is that these thoughts be considered as the business sphere develops a comprehensive set of best practices related to these three key competencies.

Notes

1. Bain & Company, <u>Bain M&A Deal Success Study</u> 4 (2004)

2. Debt leaves no wiggle room for disasters (2011) Retrieved March 15, 2011 from http://money.cnn.com/2011/03/15/news/economy/disaster_cost/index.htm

3. Malcolm Gladwell, <u>The Tipping Point: How Little Things Can Make a Big Difference</u> 12 (2002)

4. The panic has begun. What now? (2011) Retrieved March 15, 2011 from http://money.cnn.com/2011/03/15/markets/thebuzz/index.htm

5. Davos Meeting Faces Global Burnout Threat, (2011). Retrieved February 13, 2011 from http://www.reuters.com/article/2011/01/21/us-davos-idUSTRE70I41020110121

6. Ron Nielsen, <u>The Little Green Handbook</u> 104 (2006)

7. Ron Nielsen, <u>The Little Green Handbook</u> 105 (2006)

8. Ron Nielsen, <u>The Little Green Handbook</u> 110 (2006)

9. Ron Nielsen, <u>The Little Green Handbook</u> 110 (2006)

10. Ron Nielsen, <u>The Little Green Handbook</u> 110 (2006)

11. Jeffrey D. Sachs, <u>Common Wealth: Economics for a Crowded Planet</u> 153 (2008)

12. Ron Nielsen, <u>The Little Green Handbook</u> 80 (2006)

13. World Will Require 70% Growth in Farm Production by 2050 to Feed the Projected Population of 9.1 Billion. Retrieved July 31, 2010 from http://southasia.oneworld.net/globalheadlines/wake-up-call-on-future-food-crisis

14. Warnings Over Future Food Crisis, (2010). Retrieved July 31, 2010 from http://news.bbc.co.uk/2/hi/uk_news/7282196.stm

15. Ode Magazine, by Larry Gallagher, <u>Ode Magazine USA, Inc.</u> 40 (March, 2010)

16. Colony Collapse Disorder. (2010) Retrieved July 31, 2010 from http://en.wikipedia.org/wiki/colony_collapse_disorder

17. Jeffrey D. Sachs, <u>Common Wealth: Economics for a Crowded Planet</u> 23 (2008)

18. Jeffrey D. Sachs, <u>Common Wealth: Economics for a Crowded Planet</u> 17 (2008)

19. Ron Nielsen, <u>The Little Green Handbook</u> 198-199 (2006)

20. Ron Nielsen, <u>The Little Green Handbook</u> 200 (2006)

21. Ron Nielsen, <u>The Little Green Handbook</u> 205 (2006)

22. Ron Nielsen, <u>The Little Green Handbook</u> 205-206 (2006)

23. Ron Nielsen, <u>The Little Green Handbook</u> 222 (2006)

24. Warnings Over Future Food Crisis, (2010). Retrieved July 31, 2010 from http://news.bbc.co.uk/2/hi/uk_news/7282196.stm

25. Ron Nielsen, <u>The Little Green Handbook</u> 222 (2006)

26. Ron Nielsen, <u>The Little Green Handbook</u> 219 (2006)

27. U.S. Infrastructure is in Dire Straits, (2009) Retrieved January 29, 2011 from http://www.nytimes.com/2009/01/28/us/politics/28projects.html

28. Japan earthquake, tsunami likely world's costliest natural disaster at up to $309 billion (2011) Retrieved March 26, 2011 from http://www.washingtonpost.com/world/japan-earthquake-tsunami-likely-worlds-costliest-natural-disaster-at-up-to-309-billion/2011/03/22/ABR3mhFB_story.html

29. Debt leaves no wiggle room for disasters (2011) Retrieved March 15, 2011 from http://money.cnn.com/2011/03/15/news/economy/disaster_cost/index.htm

30. Jeffrey D. Sachs, <u>Common Wealth: Economics for a Crowded Planet</u> 245 (2008)

31. Jeffrey D. Sachs, <u>Common Wealth: Economics for a Crowded Planet</u> 53 (2008)

32. Chris Zook, <u>Harvard Business School Press excerpt from Beyond the Core</u> 2 (2004)

33. Chris Zook with James Allen, <u>Harvard Business School excerpt from Profit from the Core</u> 13 (2001)

34. Chris Zook, <u>Harvard Business School Press article: Finding Your Next Core Business</u> 2 (2007)

35. KPMG, <u>World Class Transactions</u> 5 (2001)

36. Chris Zook with James Allen, <u>Harvard Business School excerpt from Profit from the Core</u> 13 (2001)

37. Chris Zook, <u>Harvard Business School excerpt from Beyond the Core</u> 1 (2004)

38. Chris Zook, Harvard Business Review article: <u>Finding Your Next Core Business</u> 3 (2007)

39. Chris Zook, <u>Harvard Business School Press Book Summary of Beyond the Core</u> 2 (2004)

40. Chris Zook, <u>Harvard Business School Press excerpt from Profit from the Core</u> 2 (2006)

41. Chris Zook, <u>Harvard Business School Press excerpt from Profit from the Core</u> 10 (2004)

42. Chris Zook, <u>Harvard Business School Press excerpt from Profit from the Core</u> 2 (2004)

43. Chris Zook with James Allen, <u>Harvard Business School Press excerpt from Profit from the Core</u> 13 (2001)

44. Chris Zook with James Allen, <u>Harvard Business School excerpt from The Profitable Core</u> 35 (2001)

45. Chris Zook, <u>Harvard Business School Press article: Finding Your Next Core Business</u> 2 (2007)

46. Chris Zook, <u>Harvard Business School Press excerpt from Profit from the Core</u> 17 (2006)

47. Chris Zook with James Allen, <u>Harvard Business School excerpt from The Profitable Core</u> 3 (2001)

48. Chris Zook, Harvard Business School Press excerpt from Profit from the Core 9 (2001)

49. Chris Zook, Harvard Business School Press excerpt from Profit from the Core 3 (2001)

50. Chris Zook, Harvard Business School Press Book Summary of Beyond the Core 2 (2004)

51. Chris Zook, Harvard Business School Press Book Summary of Beyond the Core 3 (2004)

52. Chris Zook, Harvard Business School Press excerpt from Beyond the Core: Expand Your Market without Abandoning Your Roots 1 (2004)

53. Chris Zook, Harvard Business School Press Book Summary of Beyond the Core: Expand Your Market without Abandoning Your Roots 3 (2004)

54. Chris Zook and James Allen, Harvard Business Review of Growth Outside the Core 3 (2003)

55. Chris Zook, Harvard Business Review of Finding Your Next Core Business 3 (2007)

56. Chris Zook, Harvard Business Review of Finding Your Next Core Business 10 (2007)

57. Chris Zook, Harvard Business Review of Finding Your Next Core Business 11 (2007)

58. KPMG, Mergers and Acquisitions: Global Research Report 2 (1999)

59. KPMG, World Class Transactions 5 (2001)

60. KPMG, World Class Transactions 5 (2001)

61. Jeffrey D. Sachs, Common Wealth: Economics for a Crowded Planet 137 (2008)

62. Jeffrey D. Sachs, Common Wealth: Economics for a Crowded Planet 78 (2008)

63. U.S. Census Bureau. (2008) *North American Industry Classification System (NAICS)*

64. Diseconomies of Scale. (n.d.) Retrieved November 8, 2009 from the STS Wiki: http://en.wikipedia.org/wiki/Diseconomies_of_scale

65. Progressives and the Era of Trust-Busting (n.d.) Retrieved November 8, 2009 from www.fairfightfilm.org/crf/TRTrustBustingProduction

66. Progressives and the Era of Trust-Busting (n.d.) Retrieved November 8, 2009 from www.fairfightfilm.org/crf/TRTrustBustingProduction

67. Federal Trade Commission. (2008). *FTC Guide to the Antitrust Laws.*

68. KPMG, World Class Transactions 5 (2001)

69. Chris Zook and James Allen, Harvard Business Review of Growth Outside the Core 3 (2003)

70. Stephen G. Hannaford, Market Domination: The Impact of Industry Consolidation on Competition, Innovation, and Consumer Choice 3 (2007)

71. Peter Dicken, Global Shift: Mapping the Changing Contours of the World Economy 108 (2007)

72. Procurement Leaders. *10% of Daimler and BMW parts can be shared.* (2009) Retrieved September 6, 2010 from http://www.procurementleaders.com/news/latestnews/139-daimler-bmw-parts-shared/

73. Procurement Leaders. *PepsiCo and Anheuser-Busch seal procurement deal.* (2010) Retrieved September 6, 2010 from http://www.procurementleaders.com/news/latestnews/277-pepsico-anheuser-busch-deal/

74. Procurement Leaders. *Boston businesses team up to buy energy more cheaply.* (2009) Retrieved September 6, 2010 from http://www.procurementleaders.com/news/latestnews/332-businesses-buy-energy-cheap/

75. Canpotex *The Company.* Retrieved September 6, 2010 from http://canpqlx.sasktelwebhosting.com/company.htm

76. AMCOT. Retrieved September 6, 2010 from http://www.amcot. org/

77. All Business. *Bluescope Signs Joint Technical Collaboration Agreement With Nippon Steel For Next-Generation Coated Steel* (2010) Retrieved September 6, 2010 from http://www.allbusiness.com/company-activities-management/product-management/14865913-1.html

78. Findlaw. *Technical Collaboration Agreement – Sharp Corp. andUTStarcom Inc* (2000) Retrieved September 6, 2010 from http:// contracts.corporate.findlaw.com/operations/jv/5025.html

79. AMEinfo. *Gami and Hitachi sign technical collaboration agreement for the manufacturing of chilled water air conditioning equipment.* (2006) Retrieved September 6, 2010 from http://www.ameinfo. com/76140.html

80. All Business. *Horizontal cooperation in transport and logistics.* (2007) Retrieved September 6, 2010 from http://www.allbusiness.com/ operations/shipping/4509104-1.html

81. Federal Trade Commission. (2008). *FTC Guide to the Antitrust Laws.*

82. U.S. Census Bureau. (2008) *North American Industry Classification System (NAICS)*

83. Eamon Javers, (2009) *Bailouts Could Cost U.S. $23 Trillion.* Retrieved November 14, 2009 from http://dyn.politico.com

84. Jeffrey D. Sachs, Common Wealth: Economics for a Crowded Planet 245 (2008)

85. Center for Responsible Nanotechnology. *What is Nanotechnology?* Retrieved November 8, 2009 from www.crnano.org/ whatis.htm

86. Biology Online. (2006) *Genetic Engineering Advantages & Disadvantage.* Retrieved November 8, 2009 from www.biology-online. org/2/13_genetic_engineering.htm

87. Ross Reinhold. (2006). *Personality Development & Myers-Briggs MBTI Theory.* Retrieved November 15, 2009 from www. personalitypathways.com/faces.html

88. Robin Hahnel, Economic Justice and Democracy: From Competition to Cooperation 94-95 (2005)

89. World Population. (2009). Retrieved November 8, 2009 from http://en.wikipedia.org/wiki/World_population

90. World Population. (2009). Retrieved November 8, 2009 from http://en.wikipedia.org/wiki/World_population

91. UVa Today, (2009) *No One factor can Cause, Cure Economic Crisis, Experts Explain*. Retrieved November 14, 2009 from www.virginia.edu/uvatoday/newsRelease.php

92. Jeffrey D. Sachs, Common Wealth: Economics for a Crowded Planet 295 (2008)

93. Bain & Company, Bain M&A Deal Success Study 4 (2004)

94. Wikia Philosophy-Human Science. *Part and Whole*. (n.d.). Retrieved November 8, 2009 from http://humanscience.wikia.com/wiki/Part_and_Whole

95. Paul H. Ray and Sherry Ruth Anderson, The Cultural Creatives 61 (2000)

96. Paul H. Ray and Sherry Ruth Anderson, The Cultural Creatives 61 (2000)

97. Cultural Creatives (2010) Retrieved May 17, 2010 from www.kheper.net/topics/postmaterialism/cultural_creatives.html

98. Patricia Aburdene, *Megatrends 2010* 21 (2005)

99. Paul H. Ray and Sherry Ruth Anderson, The Cultural Creatives 4 (2000)

100. Paul H. Ray and Sherry Ruth Anderson, The Cultural Creatives 78 (2000)

101. Malcolm Gladwell, The Tipping Point: How Little Things Can Make a Big Difference 12 (2002)

102. The Tipping Point (2010) Retrieved May 15, 2010 from http://en.wikipedia.org/wiki/The_Tipping_Point

103. A Study of History (2010) Retrieved July 12, 2010 from http://en.wikipedia.org/wiki/A_Study_of_History

104. A Study of History (2010) Retrieved July 12, 2010 from http://en.wikipedia.org/wiki/A_Study_of_History

105. "Only Thing We Have to Fear is Fear Itself" (n.d.) Retrieved May 22, 2010 from http://historymatters.gmu.edu/d/5057/

106. Psychological Projection (2010) Retrieved August 1, 2010 from http://en.wikipedia.org/wiki/Psychological_projection

107. Zygmunt Bauman, Globalization: The Human Consequences 71 (1998)

108. Progressives and the Era of Trust-Busting (n.d.) Retrieved November 8, 2009 from www.fairfightfilm.org/crf/TRTrustBustingProduction

109. Knowledgerush. *Communism*. Retrieved November 15, 2009 from www.knowledgerush.com/kr/encyclopedia/Communisim

110. Merriam-Webster's Online Dictionary. *Main Entry: Socialism*. Retrieved November 15, 2009 from www.merriam-webster.com/dictionary/Socialism

111. All Business Dictionary of Business Terms. *Business Definition for: Central Planning*. Retrieved November 15, 2009 from www.allbusiness.com/glossaries/central-planning

112. Robin Hahnel, Economic Justice and Democracy: From Competition to Cooperation 94-95 (2005)

113. InvestorWords.Com. *Capitalism Definition*. Retrieved November 15, 2009 from www.investorwords.com/713/capitalism.html

114. Robin Hahnel, Panic Rules 68 (1999)

115. Alvin and Heidi Toffler, Revolutionary Wealth 20-23 (2006)

116. Patricia Aburdene, Megatrends 2010 45 (2005)

117. Patricia Aburdene, Megatrends 2010 21 (2005)

118. Patricia Aburdene, Megatrends 2010 45 (2005)

119. Patricia Aburdene, Megatrends 2010 45 (2005)

120. David Schweickart, After Capitalism 168 (2002)

121. Michael Albert, <u>Parecon: Life After Capitalism</u> 87 (2003)

122. Robin Hahnel, <u>Economic Justice and Democracy: From Competition to Cooperation</u> 189-194 (2005)

123. Robin Hahnel, <u>Economic Justice and Democracy: From Competition to Cooperation</u> 189-194 (2005)

124. David Schweickart, <u>After Capitalism</u> 18 (2002)

125. Jeanne N. Knutson, <u>The Human basis of the Polity</u> 29 (1972)

126. Jeffrey D. Sachs, <u>Common Wealth: Economics for a Crowded Planet</u> 78 (2008)

127. Chris Zook / James Allen, <u>Profit From the Core: Growth Strategy in an Era of Turbulence</u> 39 (2001)

128. Chris Zook / James Allen, <u>Profit From the Core: Growth Strategy in an Era of Turbulence</u> 32 (2001)

129. Chris Zook / James Allen, <u>Profit From the Core: Growth Strategy in an Era of Turbulence</u> 32 (2001)

130. Chris Zook / James Allen, <u>Profit From the Core: Growth Strategy in an Era of Turbulence</u> 32 (2001)

131. Chris Zook / James Allen, <u>Profit From the Core: Growth Strategy in an Era of Turbulence</u> 50 (2001)

132. Chris Zook / James Allen, <u>Profit From the Core: Growth Strategy in an Era of Turbulence</u> 50 (2001)

133. Chris Zook / James Allen, <u>Profit From the Core: Growth Strategy in an Era of Turbulence</u> 24 (2001)

134. Chris Zook / James Allen, <u>Profit From the Core: Growth Strategy in an Era of Turbulence</u> 24 (2001)

135. Chris Zook / James Allen, <u>Profit From the Core: Growth Strategy in an Era of Turbulence</u> 32 (2001)

136. Chris Zook, <u>Harvard Business School Press excerpt from Beyond the Core</u>: Expand Your Market without Abandoning Your Roots 1 (2004)

Index

www.ingramcontent.com/pod-product-compliance
Lightning Source LLC
Chambersburg PA
CBHW072347200326
41519CB00015B/3687